D0734619

SECRETS
FOR HUNTING
BIG BUCKS

SECRETS FOR HUNTING BIG BUCKS

How To Take Whitetails In Heavily Hunted Areas

Scott Bestul

The Lyons Press
Guilford, CT
An imprint of The Globe Pequot Press

In fond memory of Jim Thieding and David Bestul, beloved cousins,
wonderful friends, and great sportsmen who lived for the hunt . . .
and left the deer woods long before their seasons should have ended.

The Lyons Press is an imprint of The Globe Pequot Press.

10 9 8 7 6 5 4 3 2 1

Printed in The United States of America

Designed by Compset

Library of Congress Cataloging-in-Publication data
Bestul, Scott.
    Secrets for hunting big bucks / Scott Bestul.
        p. cm.
    ISBN 1-59228-101-X (alk. paper)
    1.   White-tailed deer hunting.   I. Title.
    SK301.B48 2003
    799.2'7652—dc21
                                                              2003014289

ACKNOWLEDGMENTS

No one ever writes a book by himself. To that end, I'd like to thank the following people for their invaluable contributions:

- First and foremost: Shari, Brooke, and Bailey, who sacrificed family time so I could research and write.
- Jay Cassell, who not only trusted me to write this book, but bought my first magazine article more years ago than either of us cares to admit!
- Grant Woods, James Kroll, Larry Marchinton, Brian Root, Scott Hyngstrom, Dennis Simon, John Ozoga, Karl Miller, and all the wonderful, dedicated research biologists who've been willing to share their life's work with me.
- Ron Bice, Jeff Below, Neil and Craig Dougherty, Don and Kandi Kisky, Rob Lucas, Stan Potts, Kevin Small, John Spiegl, and Bill Vaznis for sharing their time, expertise, and deer hunting stories!
- Dick Bernier and Charlie Alsheimer, wonderful, inspiring men who keep Our Creator front and center in their daily lives.
- Pat Reeve, for his friendship, photographs, and willingness to help whenever I've asked.
- Ted Marum, as fine a friend as I've had and a true student of the whitetail who has never forgotten that, above all else, deer hunting is supposed to be fun!

- Cousin Scott and the entire Bestul Hunting Crew, a large assembly of cousins, uncles, and generally good folk who keep me connected to a clan and its land each year.
- My father, the man who took me to the woods many years ago and remains my favorite hunting partner.

CONTENTS

Introduction 1

1   Defining and Assessing Pressure 9

2   What Science Says About Pressured Deer 29

3   Scouting: The Building Blocks for Success 53

4   Stand-Hunting Tactics 83

5   Still-Hunting and Tracking Techniques 113

6   Bowhunting Tactics 141

7   Driving Techniques 169

8   The Suburban/Metro Challenge 199

9   The Future: Adopting a Pressured Deer Ethic 223

INTRODUCTION

I had never heard a whitetail approach so silently before. The pair of Wisconsin deer—a mature, long-nosed doe leading the largest 8-point buck I would see for many seasons—ghosted from a stand of white pines like apparitions. I sat thirty yards away, my young posterior planted on a frigid egg-shaped chunk of granite. Moving seemed impossible; the deer had approached off my right shoulder while I looked to my left. When I'd jerked my head toward the doe she was eyeballing me and nervously shifting her front legs. The buck, like so many I would encounter in the years to come, kept his focus on his companion. In a time of danger, with gunshots sounding near and far, he trusted her to be his eyes and ears.

I had never shot at a buck before that day, and I didn't think I was going to shoot at this one. When you are twelve years old and shivering through the morning of your first deer hunt, success is something you only dreamed about the night before, with the covers pulled under your chin and your father snoring in the next bunk. Raising the barrel of that 12-gauge Model 1100 seemed as monumental a feat as kicking the winning field goal in the Super Bowl, although if you'd given me the choice between icing that game and tagging this buck, I'd have taken the whitetail without a second thought. I don't remember wanting a whole lot as a preteen, except to become a deer hunter like my father and uncles and cousins who went to the woods for a week each fall and talked of nothing else for the rest of the year.

Suddenly, though, the doe took her gaze off me and snapped her head back to glance over her shoulder. The buck did the same. And in the next few seconds an absolute miracle happened; the deer forgot about the small, trembling lump only one hundred feet away and began to walk again. As they slid behind a large aspen tree I somehow mounted the gun. When the buck stepped out I could see an ivory bead appear behind his shoulder. Then the buck's front legs sort of folded under him, and I remember thinking in that split second that maybe he had stumbled or was going to bed down for some reason—until I heard the roar of my gun and realized that I had done the thing I had set out to do.

I walked toward the buck, my legs trembling worse than I could ever remember. But later, when my father approached from behind and squeezed my shoulder, they shook even harder. Dad was chortling about the deer but looking at me, and when he extended his hand to shake mine, I felt as mixed up as I'd ever felt in my young life. There was a buck lying in the snow and I had killed it; something that was both more wonderful and terrible than I'd ever imagined. The little boy in me alternately felt like doing a silly dance or crying there in the woods, but Dad's firm grip drew me gently out of a child's world and welcomed me into another one: the fellowship of whitetail hunters. That world is one I've been a proud member of for the last thirty years.

In the days that followed my success, my father and I retold the story to anyone who'd sit still long enough. But as I listened to Dad, it was clear to me that while the tales we told ended the same way, they took different paths getting there. This much we agreed on: By 9:00 I was not only freezing, but deerless. Following his tracks in the snow, I found my dad's stand. He'd seen several deer, but no bucks. Dad was cold, too, so he walked me back toward our car to thaw out. After some hot chocolate, he pointed me toward a big round rock and told me to sit there and wait.

"I'll make a big circle through the trees in there," he said, motioning toward the woods marking the northern horizon. "Maybe I can kick something toward you."

This is where our tales diverged. When Dad heard my shot, he assumed that I'd pulled the trigger on a deer he'd pushed to me. But the truth was, my buck and doe were running *into* Dad's drive, bumped toward us by other hunters. That's why the deer had turned to look back over their shoulders; they'd heard the people who'd put them on the lam the first time, and they were ready to move out again. This was also why the doe had forgotten me for the few seconds it took to get a shot off.

When I finally explained this to Dad I could tell he was a little hurt, like I'd robbed him of an assist. But being the gentleman he is, he only shrugged his shoulders and laughed, his pride in me still strong. I had my buck, and that was what mattered.

Indeed, getting a buck was all that mattered to most of our — and everyone else's — clan in those days. Our family property, homesteaded by my great-grandfather when he arrived from Norway in the 1800s, was located in Waupaca County, Wisconsin. If you look in the state harvest records for the period from the late 1960s through the better part of the 1980s you'll notice that this county was a perennial harvest leader. This is because there were not only plenty of deer, but also plenty of people hunting them.

Hunters are notorious for flocking to hot spots, and Waupaca County fairly glowed in those years. The passion for deer hunting still burns strong there, but it's a different kind of love than it was when I was a kid. These days, most Waupaca County hunters cherish whitetails with the same deep, abiding fondness a husband has for his wife of fifty years. In the 1970s, we looked at deer like a young man leers at his bride on their wedding night.

This conquest mentality led to a carnival atmosphere that was both exciting and scary. At 6:30 on opening morning—the understood legal shooting time—sirens would peal from town halls. It was expected that at least a dozen shots would precede the sirens each year, many fired in total darkness.

By the time the sun hit the eastern treetops, the shooting would become so intense that it was pointless to count individual shots. The reports would reach a crescendo about midmorning, then tail off until noon, when everyone broke for lunch. By after-noon the gunfire would resound in isolated but intense pockets, usually as groups gathered to drive deer. I was well into my twen-ties before I thought it odd that we heard at least one ambulance every opening weekend.

The problem with such a frenetic atmosphere is that it's contagious. And for many years my family had the fever as badly as anyone. We'd sit on stand for a few hours each morning and then take the hunt to the deer. We made one-man "circles" and two- or three-hunter "pushes" or surrounded a lake with a dozen cousins, or pushed a hundred-acre swamp with every man we could enlist, some of whom we'd never even met before.

We hunted to fill tags, and most of the deer we put them on had been jumped during a drive or flushed toward security cover by another party. By the time I'd notched ten years in the white-tail woods, I couldn't have filled a daypack with my knowledge of rubs or scrapes. But I was a Ph.D. candidate in hunting pressured whitetails.

Like many deer hunters, I relive the memory of my first buck, and my early years of hunting, on a frequent basis. These were seminal years in my life, and they shaped me both as a person and as a sportsman. But even as I grew older and my approach—and indeed, the approach of our entire hunting group—toward whitetail hunting changed and evolved, I had no way of knowing what an important foundation had been laid.

I make my living as a writer now, and much of that writing is focused on whitetail deer and how to hunt them. It's a wonderful job, one that allows me to hunt more than I ever could have in most occupations. And, thanks to my career, I've had the privilege to see some outstanding deer ground; places where hunting pressure is limited and deer populations are carefully managed. Visiting those wonderful haunts—if even for a short time—is like a dream to me, an undeniable perk that's part of the occupation I'm blessed to have.

But hunting regularly in those protected deer havens is not my reality. I live with my family in a modest country home, and our income is decidedly middle class. Consequently, I do most of my hunting close to home, on land where kindly farmers have granted me permission or on public tracts that I share with dozens of other deer nuts.

When I enjoy an out-of-state hunt, the conditions are similar; I usually go on my own or with a friend or two and stay in cheap motels or camp for little or nothing. We scout and hunt and make mistakes and sometimes bring home a buck during a brief but satisfying trip. Just a small group of whitetail nerds exercising their passion in the same places most other hunters enjoy.

What does all this mean? Well, simply put, I continue to hunt deer that are pursued with a vengeance from early fall until winter's brutal grip. Three or four months competing with bowhunters in treestands, ten days of gun hunters making drives, another half-month of blackpowder nuts slipping through cover. And, of course, there is collateral pressure; squirrel and rabbit chasers, as well as men (and their dogs) after grouse and woodcock, pheasant and quail, ducks and geese. Hunters all, exercising the passion we each share for our autumn rituals.

I have the opportunity to talk with many, many whitetail hunters each fall, and for most of us there are some clear deer-hunting realities. We hunt wild, free-ranging deer. We are limited by constraints of time and money and obligations that range from the drudgery of work to the blessings of family. We must bring all our hunting knowledge of whitetails—and other hunters—to bear in those brief but wonderful hours when we escape to the woods. And though we yearn for success, we're often content just to have hunted well and safely and ethically in those precious outings.

There are more whitetail deer roaming the North American continent today than at any time in recorded history. There are also more whitetail deer hunters than ever before. This book is about finding hunting success in such an environment and about searching out new hunting opportunities in areas other hunters overlook. I hope it will be both informative and entertaining. But most of all, I hope that it will serve as a reminder of the precious gift that is deer hunting.

When I was a young boy, I read an article whose author called the whitetail buck "everyman's trophy." The writer's premise was that anyone with enough time and money could bag a trophy elk or moose or sheep, but a mature whitetail couldn't be bought. Those times—in light of the wealthy folks who pay thousands of dollars to shoot a prime whitetail on a carefully managed ranch—are long gone. But this book is not for people who can afford to "buy" a buck. It's for the Joe Lunchbuckets of the world; men and women who, like me, continue to chase the dream of a mature buck harvested through nothing more than hard work, hunting skill, and a little luck. That dream is still alive, and despite the hunting pressure we must contend with, it's still attainable.

Let's discover how to make it happen.

1

DEFINING AND ASSESSING PRESSURE

This past November, my friend Ted Marum invited me to hunt his farm during the opening weekend of the Wisconsin firearms season. I accepted for three reasons: Ted's land is only an hour from my home in Minnesota, so I could return to my family at night; I enjoy hunting with Ted and his son Jordan; and there are some dandy bucks living on my friend's place.

The week before the gun opener, I'd been bowhunting this same farm and had a mature buck within spitting distance. As so often happens in bowhunting, the buck slipped past my ambush unscathed. But the sight of that black-faced, heavy-beamed buck lit a fire under me. That same whitetail—or another like him—

could show up again during the gun season and my story might have a happier ending.

Work obligations kept me from scouting and hanging a stand before our hunt. So in the inky darkness of opening morning I packed a portable treestand, a Thompson/Center Hawken muzzleloader, and a well-stocked daypack and followed Jordan as he climbed a slim trail into the hill country. We met Ted at the base of a steep bluff.

After letting me catch my breath, Ted pointed toward a shadowy ridgeline far above us. "You need to get to the peak of that hill," my friend whispered. "There are some gnarly old oaks up there where you can hang your stand. There's all kinds of sign below the ridge—big rubs and deep trails—but ignore it.

Portable stands allow hunters to adjust to the shifting patterns of highly pressured deer. (Pat Reeve photo)

You want to be right on top; that's where the bucks go when they get pushed."

After wishing my companions luck, I made my hike. It was below freezing that morning, and the wind whipping against the bluff made it feel even colder. But I was sweating heavily by the time I'd crawled to the top of the ridge. While I rested and cooled off, I peered through the dim light at the silhouettes of trees. Picking a slim, multi-trunk red oak that still held its leaves, I screwed in a half-dozen tree steps and climbed fifteen feet. My stand fit nicely between the trunks, and after belting myself in and hauling up my gear, I settled in to wait.

The setup seemed ideal. If, as Ted predicted, the deer being pressured from below would head for this isolated ridgetop to bed, it would be very hard for them to detect me. The leafy oak tree hid my stand perfectly, and because I was on the very peak of the ridge, the wind blew my scent out over the valley. Unless I made some errant noise or the wind suddenly shifted, I felt I was sitting securely in the driver's seat.

As dawn broke, the morning's first shots echoed off the wooded bluffs. Western Wisconsin is breathtakingly beautiful country, and I spent some time soaking up the view; I could see two miles in one direction and at least twice that in another. The oak- and hickory-covered hillsides glowed bronze as the sunlight struck them, and the glens and valleys were in purple-black shadow. Flocks of sheet-white tundra swans whistled to each other as they flew toward sheltered backwaters of the Mississippi River. Although the morning was still young, I felt that my non-resident license had already paid for itself.

I sensed the deer long before I saw them. I knew the wind would mask any sounds made by approaching whitetails, so I grabbed my binoculars and started scanning the woods on the downhill side of my stand. Though I could see no deer, I kept training the glasses on a patch of blackberry brush one hundred yards away. The branches and vines were swaying in the wind, but one set of leaves was out of sync with the breeze. Finally, on my fourth glance, I discovered why; a doe was nibbling leaves from the blackberry patch, and every time she took a bite, the thick, prickly stem would bob and dance. Since I carried two tags and one was good for an antlerless deer, I kept my focus on the doe and hoped she would approach for a shot.

One of my closest friends, a highly successful trophy hunter, is fond of saying, "Every time I see a big buck, it surprises me." I would recall this phrase in a few moments when I trained the binocs on the doe again and spotted a wall of tall, ivory tines in the brush behind her. All thoughts of filling my doe tag vanished when I saw this buck. I couldn't see his antlers well enough to estimate a score, but it was clear he would make the "Bestul Book" with many inches to spare.

It took the pair of deer nearly twenty minutes to cover the short distance between us, but they behaved just as Ted said they would, ignoring the deeply worn sidehill trails and moving steadily toward the ridgetop. Although both deer were feeding, the doe was perpetually nervous, looking around and pricking her ears, robbed of her hearing by the wind. The buck nibbled leaves and acorns and rubbed his arching rack on saplings. And like my first buck many years before, he glanced frequently toward the doe, relying completely on his companion to detect danger.

At fifty steps, the buck turned broadside and stuck his nose between two trees. If he stepped further into this opening I felt I had a clear shot. But before I raised the muzzleloader I looked through the binoculars again, double-checking for brush. And just as I confirmed a clear path, the buck slipped suddenly through the lane and stepped into another tangle.

I kicked myself for messing up a solid opportunity, but I had little time for a harsh scolding, as the doe—which I'd ignored for many minutes—appeared off to my right at twenty yards. The buck must have located her about the same instant I did, because he made his first hasty move since I'd spotted him, trotting toward me for a few steps to catch up with his companion.

I honestly can't remember how many whitetails I've shot with that old Hawken rifle, but it's been a few. And this shot was a mirror image of the others; a carefully aimed bead settled into the backsight and held tight to the buck's shoulder; the gentle squeeze of the trigger, followed by a roar and a cloud of smoke. Then the nearly hopeless sense that if you've missed there is almost nothing you can do about it.

When I pulled the trigger the monster 9-point was a scant twenty-eight steps away. Then I lost him in the fog of belching sulfur. When he reappeared he was standing only forty yards away, looking around for whatever had made that awful sound. I was convinced I'd blown it and was making a mental checklist of where my powder, shot, and caps were stashed when the buck staggered ten steps downhill and died.

In many ways, killing that buck brought me full circle. Though the hunting pressure surrounding my friend's Wisconsin farm was nothing like I'd witnessed in my early years, it was definitely a factor in moving the deer. Indeed, Ted's only advice that morning spoke volumes about our hunting conditions: "Ignore the deer sign and go where the bucks go when they're being pushed."

Hunters who understand how deer react to intense pressure can still score on bucks like this one. (Pat Reeve photo)

The underlying assumption of that statement forms the cornerstone of hunting pressured whitetails. We are pursuing animals that, for one or more reasons, have changed their normal routines to adapt to a predatory influence. How successfully we adapt to those changes often determines our hunting success.

Whitetail adaptations to hunting pressure can be subtle or dramatic, depending on the situation. It is only natural, of course, for whitetails to be elusive and secretive. They are a prey species that has refined its survival instincts over centuries of predation. In Nature's design, an unwary deer is often a dead one. However, things are different now than when *Odocoileus virginiana* first assumed its role on the North American landscape. There are fewer mammalian predators than there were even a hundred years ago. Wolves, except in a very few states, are no longer part of the landscape. Mountain lion populations have been greatly reduced over their traditional range. Coyotes are certainly a whitetail predator, as are black bears and bobcats, but since the effect these animals have on whitetail populations in most areas is relatively small, humans remain the most significant predator.

How deer respond to the presence of humans varies greatly. There are certainly areas where whitetails worry little about people. Urban parks and reserves are the most obvious examples, as are other sanctuaries where hunting is prohibited. But even in some huntable areas, whitetails may see such limited pressure that they have little to fear from humans. Because of difficult or

In places where hunting access is restricted, deer often remain much more relaxed when humans are around.

restricted access, deer may have encounters with only a handful of hunters each year. In such instances, whitetails seem almost naive.

I once visited a 1,500-acre estate in the Midwest owned by a wealthy family in California that refused to allow hunting. Despite moderate to intense hunting pressure on the lands adjoining this property, the whitetails living on the protected acreage seemed largely oblivious to the presence of humans. Mature bucks could be seen nibbling on apple trees in the middle of the day. Does and fawns would bed down close to roads and barely turn their heads when a car drove by. There were no high fences, no feeding programs, and no pen-raised animals; just a pocket of sanctuary in a sea of chaos. Whitetails had, as always, simply adapted their behavior to suit the environment.

Hunters who are willing to work hard are usually the most successful.

On the other end of the spectrum there are states like Wisconsin, Michigan, Pennsylvania, Alabama, and Mississippi, where whitetail hunting is not just a sport, it's a way of life. Schools shut down for the first week of the firearms season. Factories and businesses offer furlough programs or schedule shutdowns to accommodate whitetail addicts. Small-town hotels, restaurants, and retail businesses may make more money during the deer season than they do during peak summer vacation time. And residents sponsor events where the term "hunter" is used as an adjective instead of a noun—hunter's ball, hunter's breakfast, hunter's raffle. And everyone knows that a hunter's widow hasn't lost her spouse forever, just until January. In places like these, whitetails experience intense hunting pressure from their five-month birthday until the day they die, a date that may arrive sooner rather than later.

In between the extremes of total sanctuary and statewide assault, there are varying degrees of hunting pressure. I have both lived and hunted in Iowa, a state considered by many to be the nation's finest for taking a trophy whitetail buck. The Hawkeye State is, in many respects, a deer hunter's paradise. The herd is healthy and abundant, mature bucks are present in decent numbers (you'll notice I do not use the terms "common" or "easy to kill"), and access to prime private land is possible.

Having bowhunted several other states, I would rate the pressure in Iowa low to moderate, depending on the location. (I should add that as a teenager I cut my bowhunting teeth on a tract of Iowa public ground where I would rate the pressure as "insane." So my low-to-moderate gauge is applied as a statewide average.) This makes whitetails relatively naïve during Iowa's archery season, compared to, say, deer living in Wisconsin.

There are simply fewer hunters afield and fewer disturbances for deer going about their daily routines.

But come December—when the statewide shotgun seasons open—Iowa becomes a different world. Because those firearms seasons are relatively brief, hunters pursue whitetails intensely. Drives are organized and brush is pushed. Ditches and creek bottoms, old farmsteads, and isolated blocks of timber that have not seen a person in months are suddenly awash in blaze orange. And, not surprisingly, whitetails quickly recall the survival lessons that were hard-wired into their beings at birth.

Want to see a majestic, swaggering trophy whitetail undergo a character transformation? Watch a dozen hunters blitz his bedroom. That once proud monarch morphs into a skulking cottontail or a speeding antelope in seconds and doesn't change his demeanor for many, many days.

Since there are so many varieties and levels of hunting pressure, let's set some simple definitions. But before we do, let me state that I don't believe that any wild, free-ranging deer is free from pressure and, therefore, completely naive. When I stated earlier that the unhunted deer on that Midwestern estate didn't seem to view people as a threat, I was observing them from a car. To these whitetails, our behavior was the accepted, "natural" behavior of humans. Had we stopped the vehicle and walked toward the deer, they would have undoubtedly run off. A walk through the surrounding woods would have put the deer on even higher alert.

Would the reactions of these whitetails have equaled those of deer living in a hard-hunted area? Certainly not. But I'm equally certain that just a few encounters with hunters in treestands or even a few days of small drives would have educated these deer in a hurry. As I've mentioned, whitetails are a prey species, and evading predators does not require a long learning curve. As my old high school biology teacher would have said, "It's in their genes."

That said, let's look at some levels of pressure, starting with the least intense.

Level One pressure includes whitetails that are seldom or rarely hunted. This can include deer residing in parks, refuges or preserves, metro/suburban woodlots and green spaces, and relatively large properties where hunting is not allowed. I'd also include whitetails living in areas open to hunting where large tracts of difficult terrain (mountains, big woods, swamps, etc.) prevent hunters from accessing them except for brief periods, if at all. Not all wilderness-type settings qualify as Level One, though. In my home state of Minnesota, for example, there are square miles of northwoods timber that rarely see a hunter. However, there are healthy populations of timber wolves residing in these areas, and whitetails live on high alert every day of their lives.

Level Two pressure includes areas where deer experience only limited hunting pressure in the course of a season. These can include private properties where hunter numbers are severely restricted by the landowner, public areas that receive light to moderate numbers of hunters due to difficult terrain or limited-entry quotas, or perhaps a military base that hosts a brief hunt each fall to help thin the deer herd. While whitetails living on such properties "wise up" in a hurry to the presence of hunters, they spend the majority of their lives without the constant threat of predation.

Level Three pressure includes properties where hunters pursue deer on a consistent basis throughout the fall. Some peaks of high hunter activity may be seen, such as during firearms seasons. The majority of private properties, where landowners allow hunting to occur but limit the number of participants, would qualify. Larger public areas, or those lying some distance from a major metropolitan area or population center, might also fit the definition.

Level Four constitutes the highest level of hunting pressure that whitetails face. Deer living in these areas are pursued rigorously throughout the hunting season, from the early archery and muzzleloader opening through the last days of the season. Access to private properties is liberal or unrestricted, and public lands—which are relatively small and close to major population centers—are heavily hunted. Under such a scenario, whitetails become masters of evasion or they are turned into venison. Does earn a graduate degree in detecting and avoiding hunters by their second or third season. Mature bucks (assuming there are any) are almost vampires, traveling and feeding, fighting and breeding largely under the cover of darkness.

If you've hunted a particular piece of property for many seasons, chances are you'd have little trouble fitting your situation into one of the definitions listed above. And, of course, it's entirely possible for one property to see a shift in the pressure level within the course of a single fall.

One farm close to my home that I've been bowhunting for the last couple of seasons is a perfect example. When archery season opens in mid-September, the deer on this property are fairly relaxed and remain so throughout the early bow season. This is because the landowner severely limits the number of hunters—including firearms hunters—on his property. But once the gun

Evaluating the level of pressure on the land you plan to hunt allows you to devise a solid hunting strategy before the season even starts. (Pat Reeve photo)

season begins, the deer undergo a transformation similar to the shift I mentioned that occurs in Iowa each fall. Because this farm is relatively small (500 acres), the whitetails living there receive moderate to severe pressure on the adjoining lands, which are also part of their home range.

When I visit this farm after the firearms season, I'm always amazed at how razor-sharp the senses of these deer have become. Let a mature doe get even a hint of human presence—from whiffing a boot track on an entry trail to spotting an odd silhouette in a tree—and the hunt is over in seconds. I've watched a doe spend long minutes sniffing where I brushed against a branch or staring intently into the treetops until she spotted me.

One month earlier I could get away with a small mistake, but following the gunning season even the tiniest gaffe is not only recognized, it's announced to the entire herd.

For hunters new to a property or for those seeking to hunt in an unfamiliar area, assessing the amount of pressure the area receives can be invaluable. Not only will such an assessment help you decide on potential tactics, it can help you define legitimate goals for the season. For example, if I feel a new area is experiencing Level Four pressure, I'll probably place treestands closer to bedding areas, as daytime deer movement will occur only at the last sliver of light. Similarly, knowing the number of mature bucks in the herd is likely to be low, I'd probably not expect to have as many—and perhaps no—big-buck encounters in the course of a season. Such knowledge would help me make a reasonable decision about the size of the buck I'd attempt to harvest. Holding out for a monster whitetail in an area where they don't exist is nothing but a recipe for frustration.

So how do you assess the pressure levels on a particular property? Like most everything else about successful deer hunting, hard work and ingenuity are essential. If I'm lucky enough to access private land, I typically quiz the landowner about the behavior and habits of other hunters (if any) that visit his farm. I want to know the numbers of hunters, when they typically visit (weekends, weekdays, gun or bow season, etc.), and the areas they tend to hunt. This not only gives me an idea of how much pressure the property receives, but when and how it occurs. Such information helps me develop a strategy to focus my efforts on times and places when I'm most likely to be alone. Hunting at such times, if possible, assures me that my hunts will not only be more effective, but also more safe and of higher quality.

Maintaining friendly landowner relations helps secure hunting permission and may even lead to a gold mine of good information about the habits of area whitetails. (Pat Reeve photo)

For example, one property I hunted for many seasons was also used by several other whitetail hunters. In talking to the farmer, I learned the other hunters were restricted largely to weekend trips. I had the luxury of hunting this place whenever I wanted, and at first I did so. But after looking at my journal from that first season, I learned that fully 80 percent of my buck sightings occurred on hunts from Tuesday through Friday. By Saturday, buck encounters had tailed off significantly, and on Sundays, after a full weekend of hunter contact, the bucks were tallying a lot of marks in the "skunked" column of my journal. The next fall I hunted this farm only on weekdays.

If the landowner isn't sure about the behavior of other hunters or if you're hunting public property, it's usually a safe bet to assume that most pressure will occur on weekends. Deciphering the patterns of other hunters, however, takes more time and legwork. Usually, I like to make several scouting trips to the property, looking to establish hunter patterns as much as find deer sign. I look for human entry and exit trails leading from likely parking places into the timber, treestands and/or steps left from previous seasons, and human sign around the patches of cover lying closest to roads and parking lots. While it's an oft-repeated cliché that most hunters simply will not walk very far from a vehicle, my experience has shown this to be largely true.

Sometimes it's possible to make at least a partial assessment of pressure without visiting an area at all. If you know, for example, that hunter numbers are limited by license quotas, season structure, or large blocks of difficult-to-access habitat, you can assume that hunting pressure will diminish, as well. Drawing a tag for a limited-entry hunt like those held on refuges, military lands, or state parks also will insure that, in most instances, the deer will have been largely undisturbed prior to your visit.

To assess the pressure that will exist during the course of your hunt, I'd make it a point to call the hunt manager for his/her opinion on what to expect: deer numbers, habitat use, hunter behavior, and hot spots of hunter activity in the past. Sometimes just a few minutes spent chatting with such an individual can net valuable information.

Similarly, if you plan an out-of-state hunt to a place where licenses are severely limited, it's fairly reasonable to expect lower hunter numbers simply because there will be fewer nonresidents.

Bucks like this beauty can still be found on public land—if you do your homework.

However, since the number of resident hunters is rarely restricted, expect there to be pockets of pressure where landowners allow liberal access. The same goes for public grounds close to major population centers.

Let's take another look at the public hunting area in Iowa that I mentioned earlier. While there can be some outstanding deer hunting on many public tracts in the Hawkeye State (a good friend of mine has tagged two trophy bucks in as many seasons on a small state-owned tract), a state wildlife area that I bowhunted as a teenager was a disappointing exception. Although this acreage was large and contained excellent deer habitat, it was located within an easy drive of two large cities. Consequently, it received considerable hunting pressure. While I was able to arrow a decent buck there my senior year of high school, it took my buddy Tim and me a lot of walking (often in hip boots) to locate areas where deer were moving during daylight. Hunting this ground taught me that all public hunting grounds are not created equal, even in the best of states.

While it may seem like all this time spent assessing pressure is taking valuable energy and effort away from the hunting itself, I'd argue that nothing is further from the truth. By identifying the amount, timing, and nature of the human contact the whitetails on your property are receiving, you can then formulate a logical hunting plan. In doing so, you'll be able to make the most of every opportunity you have.

If, like most of us, you're not blessed with unlimited hours to spend in the woods, maximizing your effort for the time you do have is paramount. I'd rather clock three hours a week hunting a property where I know the haunts and behaviors of deer than burn half a week of nonstop effort on a farm where I'm guessing every time I hit the woods.

In short, when we assess pressure we are trying to identify times and places when deer are most vulnerable. Whitetails are not like elk, which when pressured can just put a mountain or two between themselves and danger. Instead, whitetails remain in a relatively small home range and simply adapt their behavior in order to avoid a threat.

Now, let's examine what scientists—and hunters—have discovered about the unique adaptations deer make when they know they're being hunted.

2

WHAT SCIENCE SAYS ABOUT PRESSURED DEER

It is a bitter January day in Minnesota, and I am standing in a windswept field watching the equivalent of a whitetail rodeo. From a landing zone on the bluff-country ridge, a helicopter takes off and makes a low, sweeping circle over a wooded hillside, tilted at an odd angle. Swinging back over me, the chopper repeats the process, flying slightly lower this time. Suddenly, three deer emerge from the woods, running frantically through the field to escape the noise and wind generated by the chopper.

Two of the deer quickly circle back to the woods, but a lone doe maintains her course into the open. The chopper banks hard and low, then levels off when it's hovering slightly above the doe. A man in an orange jumpsuit leans out of the chopper door. I

Helicopters allow biologists to capture whitetails for telemetry studies.

hear the light "pop" of a rifle cartridge as the orange figure shoots a special gun that sends a web of orange netting at the deer. His aim is true, and the net engulfs the running whitetail. The doe stumbles in the net, becomes entangled, and falls on her side in the snow.

The chopper lifts, makes a short loop, then sweeps close to the ground near the doe. The man in the orange suit jumps from the chopper and runs to the deer, chugging through snowdrifts while holding a bundle of ropes and a cloth in his hands. Like a calf-roper racing a stopwatch, the man plows to a stop next to the deer, quickly binding its front and hind legs together with a rope, then slides a cloth mask over her eyes. The process takes mere seconds, and the doe calms as the blindfold robs her vision. A moment later the chopper returns to hover well above the deer, a long cable dangling from its belly. The orange-clad bulldogger grabs the cable, attaches it to the rope constricting the deer's legs, then backs away quickly while signaling the chopper that he's clear. The helicopter lifts into the clear January sky, carrying the doe toward a small group of men waiting near me.

The men are Minnesota Department of Natural Resources (MDNR) researchers, and as soon as the chopper pilot has gently placed the doe on the snow and lifted away, they run to the deer. I follow, watching as they swing into action like an ER crew tending a major trauma victim. They take blood samples with a syringe, use a rectal thermometer to assess body temperature, measure neck circumference, inject the deer with an antibiotic, and fix a tag to the deer's ear. Finally, one man grabs a collar fitted with a transmitter and straps it around the doe's neck. Through the process, the whitetail remains relatively quiet, the blindfold calming her as she is handled.

These biologists attach a radio collar to a doe and then release her. By tracking deer over extended periods, scientists have learned much about deer movement and behavior.

When the group has finished its work the ropes are pulled from the doe's legs and she stands. All the researchers back away but one, who continues to hold the deer while pointing her to a woodline two hundred yards away. Then he removes the blindfold. The doe runs for a few steps, stops, then shakes her head slightly as she feels the collar. Oriented now, she trots toward the woods, sporting some new jewelry that will help MDNR biologists learn more about her life. By day's end, sixteen more deer will be captured and fitted with telemetry collars at this site. They will join dozens of other deer in a multi-year study of survival rates, causes of mortality, and annual movements of whitetails in southern Minnesota.

As a whitetail fanatic and longtime deer hunter, I've always been fascinated by research—particularly telemetry studies—involving deer. While I spend hundreds of hours each year observing deer and their sign, so much of their life remains a mystery to me—and to most other hunters. In fact, one of my enduring dreams would be to capture a grand whitetail buck, fit him with a radio collar, and spend the rest of the fall doing nothing but following him as he feeds, pursues does, and hides from hunters. Such an experience would be a fascinating glimpse into the world of a mature buck.

As I began working on this book, my fascination with research led me to ask some of the country's top deer biologists about how whitetails respond to hunting pressure. These men and women often spend more time among deer in a year than most of us do in a decade or more. And they attempt to analyze deer behavior scientifically, without the preconceived notions most of us carry along when we attempt to interpret why deer do what they do.

I started by asking for their impressions on how deer respond to hunting pressure. Interestingly, I found that little research had been devoted specifically to this topic; that is, not many scientists have designed a study that specifically addresses the question, "When hunters do this, what will deer do?" However, many biologists tracking and/or observing deer during telemetry studies have noted whitetail responses to predators, hunting (or even stray) dogs, and human activity within their home ranges. Their observations and data provide some interesting material for hunters to consider.

PATTERN SHIFTS

Dr. James Kroll, one of the country's most noted researchers and a devout whitetail hunter, says that one of the classic adaptations, especially for bucks, is to shift the timing of their movements to when they're least likely to encounter hunters.

"We've seen this time and again in bucks we've either studied or observed," he said. "And I've come to the conclusion that, as bucks age, nocturnal movement is a natural progression. One example occurred with a buck we nicknamed 'Little Tough Stuff,' a name he received because of his aggressive personality. As a one-and-a-half-year-old deer, this buck was very visible and easy to observe. But as he grew up, he began a gradual shift toward nighttime movement. By the time he was four and a half years old—and carrying a true trophy rack—ninety-five percent of his movement occurred at night.

"What's truly interesting about this shift is that Little Tough Stuff lived on a huge tract of land that received virtually no hunting pressure. So while it's easy for us to assume that deer logically respond to a human presence by moving at night, such behavior might be just a natural behavior function of growing older."

Dr. Kroll also notes that whitetails that move a lot at night may adopt another interesting behavior. "There is often a corresponding shift into a midday movement pattern as well," he says. "So where we typically view a whitetail as having peak movement times at dawn and dusk, a deer that exhibits a tendency toward nocturnal movement is also one that may have another spike of activity in the middle of the day—say from 10 AM through 2 PM—that frequently goes unobserved. In fact, whenever I advise hunters about how to hunt trophy-class whitetails, the advice I give most frequently is to stay on stand during the middle of the day. Interestingly, that is also the advice that's most frequently ignored."

Nocturnal movement is both a natural behavior and a learned survival mechanism for mature bucks. (Pat Reeve photo)

What factors put a whitetail, especially a mature buck, on his feet during the middle of the day? For starters, Dr. Kroll notes that whitetails typically need to eat about once every four hours and often have to rise from their beds to do so. The movement they make to accomplish this may be small, but could be exploited by a hunter. Dr. Kroll once hunted a mature buck that had retreated to an impenetrable sanctuary to bed by legal shooting light each morning. But after several seasons of hunting this buck, Kroll realized the whitetail was also leaving the sanctuary at midday, following a creek bottom toward one of two food sources. By staying on stand through midday for several days, Kroll finally killed the buck as it moved from its sanctuary at 11:15 AM.

Whitetails may also make a midday shift to another bedding area. This movement is often in response to a climatic change. In the South, the rising sun may bump temperatures just enough to cause a buck to rise from his original bed and move to one that is more shaded or breezy. In the North, winter whitetails frequently rise in midday to bed on a south-facing slope to take advantage of ambient sunlight and warmer temperatures. I have also had several hunting partners tell me of seeing bucks at waterholes in midday during a particularly warm spell in the fall. Presumably, these bucks were slaking their thirst after a hard night of activity, either running does or feeding heavily.

The rut, of course, is a prime time for midday deer movement. Bucks will frequently cruise through known bedding areas, seeking an estrous doe. Also, a buck that has had no success finding a willing doe among the deer living in his typical home range will often strike out cross-country to find more family groups to investigate. While this type of movement is often very difficult to time or predict, hunters who have the patience to stay on stand all day often encounter bucks they would see at no other time.

Whitetails may also shift the timing of their movements in response to human presence. For example, if whitetails are encountering hunters whenever they move at dawn and/or dusk, they may adjust their own "schedule" and become more active whenever they're least likely to bump into people. This, of course, is a classic explanation for the nocturnal movement so often adopted by mature bucks. As mentioned earlier, there are several other factors that might lead whitetails to move at night. The natural progression of bucks toward this behavior, as noted by Dr. Kroll, is one. Moon phase, weather patterns, and other environmental situations are others. But certainly daytime hunting pressure is an important consideration.

This nice buck is feeding in an open field in broad daylight. In the face of consistent pressure, deer quickly learn to alter their normal routines. (Pat Reeve photo)

As an example of a deer's ability to shift patterns to adjust to human pressure, consider the following story from biologist and researcher Grant Woods. Woods, who has studied deer across the continent and worked extensively as a deer manager, recalls being hired to reduce a whitetail herd that was destroying vegetation on an expansive golf course.

"We began our operation by killing deer at night, because that was the only time the golf course wasn't being used," Woods recalls. "Using high-power rifles and a spotlight, we killed a hundred deer in the first year. But in the following three years, it became extremely difficult to shoot even one deer using that technique. The deer had become so wary that the minute you shined a light on a distant pair of whitetail eyes, the deer would run for cover. Our fourth year we managed to kill only one female fawn."

With deer numbers on the course still in need of thinning, Woods and his team adopted a unique strategy. "We decided to hunt the midday hours, using archery equipment," he says. "We placed treestands in wooded areas adjacent to the fairways. In the first seven hours of hunting we killed six deer. Those whitetails were completely unaccustomed to not only treestands, but to encountering any type of danger during daylight hours."

While Woods's example involved the opposite of normal nocturnal deer movement (the deer became more active during daylight instead of after dark), it serves as powerful proof of the whitetail's ability to shift patterns in response to pressure.

LOCATION SHIFTS

Another whitetail response to hunting pressure is to shift their movement, or perhaps even relocate, to an area where they are less disturbed. For example, let's suppose that a buck's home range includes a large alfalfa field surrounded by prairie grass, a wooded tract of open, mature timber, and a dense swamp bisected by a shallow creek. Prior to the hunting season, the buck may use each of these areas equally, depending on his food and cover requirements.

But when hunting season begins and human activity increases, that situation may change dramatically. Let's imagine bowhunters filtering into the hardwoods, waiting for deer to feed on acorns. Pheasant hunters then start their fall by plodding through the prairie grass, looking to fill their game bags. As the buck encounters hunters in these areas, he may shift the largest percentage of his movement to the place where he's disturbed the least—the tangled swamp.

This phenomenon has been documented before, most notably in a study on Nebraska's Desoto National Wildlife Refuge. There, University of Nebraska researcher Scott Hyngstrom headed a twelve-year telemetry study that examined the movements of 150 radio-collared does. While the study was not designed to examine how deer respond to hunting pressure, Hyngstrom noted some interesting behavior during annual muzzleloader seasons.

"The Desoto is closed to whitetail hunting, with the exception of two, three-day muzzleloader seasons," Scott says. "And, unfortunately, we were not able to locate our deer at frequent intervals during those hunts, largely because we were manning check stations where hunters would register their deer."

Despite this handicap, Hyngstrom saw a dramatic response to hunters by one old doe. "We called her Doe #15," Scott recalls. "We first got a collar on her when she was six years old, so she was already pretty adept at survival. She was a matriarchal doe, which meant that she was the leader of a small group of does and fawns, composed of her offspring and theirs. Every year, as soon as the muzzleloader hunts would start, she would head directly for a small 'natural area' that was closed to hunting—indeed, human traffic—for the duration of the season.

"Though the natural area was within her home range, it typically took a significant movement—often a half mile or more—for her to get there. But she'd head for that spot every year, taking the five to fifteen deer that followed her everywhere, as soon as the shooting started. Then she'd remain largely within that spot until the hunt had ended. Within a day or two of the end of the hunt, she'd leave the natural area and return to the core of her home range."

Hyngstrom was unable to explain the uncanny survival tactic of Doe #15. "It could have been dumb luck," he quips. "But I doubt it. Perhaps she was born there and it was just instinctive for her to return. One thing I know, she was an older deer when we first captured her, which means she already had opportunity to learn about, and evade, hunting pressure. There's certainly something to be said for that. I doubt that younger deer, or deer that had never received hunting pressure, would have been as successful."

Doe #15 remained successful in avoiding hunters until she was thirteen years old, when she was killed by a sixteen-year-old boy.

"The doe was just unlucky that year," Hyngstrom says. "For some reason, the night before the muzzleloader season opened she left her core area and went off about a third of a mile to a large field. She was on her way back when the shooting started, and following a small line of brush along a creekbed to get there.

Hunters often underestimate the wariness of does.

The young hunter was set up along that cover and was able to get her. We were happy to see him get such a nice deer."

James Kroll noted similar behavior in whitetails he has studied. "Deer are very adept at identifying the areas within their home ranges where they aren't disturbed," he says. "And they are very aware of the presence of hunters who aren't careful of their noise and scent. We had one radio-collared buck that we were monitoring during the hunting season. As we tracked him, we realized he was heading right down a trail where we knew a hunter was set up. Naturally, we expected the buck to be shot, but just as the deer was getting close to the hunter, he stopped, made a wide circle, and continued right down the trail he was on. I think most hunters would be amazed at how often they're extremely close to deer."

Another hunter's trait that Kroll has observed—and one that whitetails have also learned to exploit—is a fear of getting more than 1,500 feet from a road. "We've proven this time and again," he states. "And I've used this information to help myself and other hunters find some very good deer hunting without even scouting a territory on foot. You can look at a topo map and just begin circling areas over a quarter mile from a road and then look for terrain features that deer will use to travel (creekbeds, benches, saddles in a ridge) within that area and circle them. Often you can walk right to that spot and find some great deer sign—and rarely another hunter. Deer are simply making small shifts in their home range to places where they're rarely disturbed."

THE REFUGE EFFECT

One of the most common beliefs held by deer hunters is that areas closed to hunting—state parks, natural areas, waterfowl refuges, and other game sanctuaries—are full of trophy-class bucks. But is that belief correct? Dennis Simon, a biologist with the Minnesota Department of Natural Resources, conducted an extensive telemetry study on deer living in a state game refuge. The study's main purpose—to estimate how many deer that game managers were missing in winter fly-over counts—ended up giving Simon a fascinating glimpse into how deer use refuges.

"Deer use of the refuge depended on the time of year," Simon said. "In spring and early summer, deer seemed about evenly divided between sedentary deer—those that used the refuge as their home ground—and migratory deer that left the refuge."

Simon notes that some of the migratory deer really put on their walking shoes. "We had one deer that left the refuge every spring, traveled about nine miles to the Mississippi River, swam the river, and moved into Wisconsin, where she had her fawn. In early fall she'd make the same trek back to the refuge with her fawn." Other deer made similar large movements, including a pair of yearlings that would travel up to sixteen miles in a single evening, then move back into the refuge in a day or two.

But other deer exhibited what Simon calls "site tenacity." These deer adopted territories closer to the accepted norm, about one square mile. "They would use micro-habitats within that range according to the season," Simon notes. "We had does that would drop their fawns in the same corner of the same field every spring, for example. And in winter deer used only a fraction of the habitats that suited their needs for that season; perhaps a south-facing slope that protected them from winds and had browse available."

Though less than a week old, this fawn will soon get a crash course in survival behavior from its mother. (Pat Reeve photo)

Simon concluded that whitetails adopt behaviors taught to them by their mothers. That is, if a doe "migrates," her fawns will likely repeat that behavior. The same holds true for homebody deer. In short, whitetails "learn" successful survival behaviors.

Interestingly, the refuge Simon studied was closed to human travel during the hunting season. Did the whitetails that called it home "know" it was a safe haven?

"About the same time every fall—about the opening of the small game season in September—deer that had been living outside the refuge often moved back in," he said. "Long before environmental factors like weather and food availability should influence them, deer sought out the refuge. We felt they did this in response to hunting pressure."

Simon feels that this movement in the fall is also a learned behavior. The area surrounding the refuge is a public hunting ground, and pressure on the refuge outskirts can be intense, especially during the firearms deer season.

"The 'firing line' effect on the refuge borders was pretty amazing," Simon reflects. "Basically, a deer moving out of the refuge during daylight hours didn't stand much of a chance. Neither did deer that moved continually in response to hunting pressure. So you had some natural selection going on. The deer that moved at night and/or stuck to unhunted cover survived. Those that didn't were killed." Scientifically speaking, it may be a stretch to say that whitetails "learned" to stay in the refuge, but the deer (and their offspring) that remained within the non-hunted area—at least while hunting seasons were on—lived, while those that strayed from its confines didn't.

Many hunters feel that refuges are full of adult bucks, a notion that Simon says is only partially true. "Refuges do allow some bucks to survive," he notes. "But they can only save so many. It's very difficult to stockpile trophy deer in a refuge." The reasons for this are largely related to dominance and breeding behaviors of mature bucks, Simon says. "For starters, the rut has an extremely strong influence on bucks. During the rut, bucks are constantly moving, looking for receptive does. This makes them very vulnerable. We got harvest information on a number of bucks that we had tagged during the study. Those harvest locations looked like spokes coming out of a wheel, and the hub of that wheel was the refuge.

"Dominance is another factor. The refuge we studied was only about four square miles, and in an area that size you'll only have about four or five truly adult bucks (4½ to 5½ years old) that have established dominance. Other bucks will disperse to find does. There will be some 2½- and 3½-year-old bucks remaining in the refuge, but typically you'll rarely see more than one real trophy per square mile of refuge. Every hunter believes that refuges are just full of big deer, but in the three years of our study we saw very few after the hunting season. We felt that intense hunting pressure outside the refuge was eliminating many of the big bucks every fall."

RUN OR HIDE?

Most of the information discussed so far in this chapter has dealt with a whitetail's ability to avoid minor intrusions within its home range—a relatively small number of hunters invading a whitetail's core area. But what happens when a deer is confronted with a direct and serious threat to its existence? Having come from an area where the hunting pressure—in the form of legions of standers, still-hunters, and drivers ranging from a handful to two dozen or more—I was interested to see if biologists had examined this topic.

As it turned out, there has been little research done directly on this topic, but two projects certainly are relevant to deer dealing with this type of pressure. The first occurred in northern Missouri during the mid-1980s. Brian Root, a biologist with the Missouri Department of Conservation, led a two-year telemetry study of whitetails living near the Deer Ridge Wildlife Area in Lewis County. Brian and his colleagues took telemetry locations every two hours during the nine days prior to the firearms season, then compared those movements to the days encompassed within the nine-day hunting season itself, as well as the same period following the hunt.

No matter whether they decide to run or hide, whitetails like this velvet buck learn early to use dense cover to their advantage. (Pat Reeve photo)

"Since this was a public hunting area, the pressure was pretty intense, especially on the weekends," Root says. "It's interesting to note that adjacent to the public hunting area there was a refuge that was off limits to hunters. Some of our radio-collared animals had the refuge as part of their core area, pre-hunt."

Root's research revealed that does outside the refuge increased their movement by as much as 25 percent—from an average of two and a half miles per day to over three miles per day—during the hunting season.

"They weren't leaving their home ranges at all," he notes. "They were just doing a lot more moving in response to hunting pressure. Interestingly, the does living on the refuge weren't making this shift."

Bucks, on the other hand, didn't show any increase in movement. "The hunt was scheduled right during the peak of the rut, and bucks were already moving four or five miles per day," Root recalls. "This amount of movement did not change once the hunting season began, even when hunter densities reached one hundred people per square mile. Bucks did move erratically, presumably to wait in cover to avoid a nearby hunter, but they did not stop their search for does.

"We did get to witness one buck that hunkered down in a brushy fencerow while a disgruntled hunter trudged past him. Though the hunter passed within twenty feet of the buck, the deer never moved. About ten minutes later the buck stood up, and within a couple of hours he'd traveled about a half mile."

Root noted that no deer outside the refuge made a move to get there for the apparent safety that many hunters believed the off-limits area afforded. They simply moved to avoid hunters when they had to, or as in the case of the tight-sitting buck, hunkered down to let them walk by.

Such behavior was seen on a more dramatic level during a telemetry study conducted by Georgia researcher Larry Marchinton. While studying the effects of deer hunting with hounds, Marchinton and his colleagues saw how whitetails behaved under pressure more intense than even the most carefully orchestrated drive could muster. While it serves as an extreme example, Marchinton's observations offer a revealing glimpse into the world of deer behavior.

Larry divided the responses of deer to the pursuit of dogs into three categories. The first response was "holding." If a white-

Many hunters are unaware of how frequently bucks use grassy cover like this to escape hunting pressure. (Pat Reeve photo)

tail held, Marchinton notes, "he simply remained bedded and allowed the dogs to approach within a short distance. Their ability to do this can't be underestimated. With one particular two-year-old buck, we repeatedly tried to get dogs to run him while he was holed up in a thick patch of honeysuckle. Despite being surrounded by dogs, the buck refused to run. Eventually, the dogs left the patch and began chasing another deer.

"I was sure the dogs had finally jumped the deer and it left unnoticed. But when I checked the signal, the buck was still there. I approached to within a few yards of the buck and noticed that one of the dogs had defecated about three feet from where he was hiding."

Marchinton notes that in about half of the chases, deer were able to elude dogs simply by holding.

Deer that chose to run from the hounds used two different techniques to elude them. "Some deer, particularly bucks, chose to run a relatively straight line, using their speed and endurance to outrun the pack," Marchinton recalls. "One large buck that used this escape method ran for close to thirteen miles and scattered the pack as he ran. This chase took him far from his familiar territory, of course. But within a day he had returned to his home range."

Other deer, particularly does and fawns, chose to run circuitous or zigzag patterns in an attempt to throw off the hounds. Frequently they headed for water, such as a swamp or stream, in an apparent attempt to confuse their scent trail. They also ran among other deer, presumably to mingle their scent and again confuse the hounds. When deer chose this method, they would make frequent stops, apparently to check their backtrail to determine if other animals were still following.

Marchinton was not able to determine why some deer chose to run cross-country versus taking a zigzag path when dogs chased them. "Some of it is probably dictated by cover, terrain, or the speed and/or tenacity of the pack of dogs itself," he says. "But certainly some of it seems to be the way an individual deer responds to pressure."

Marchinton notes that whitetails were far more likely to hold in extremely dense cover when they encountered dogs.

FINAL THOUGHTS

How does such information benefit hunters? In the case of Larry Marchinton's research, it should help hunters understand how whitetails respond to a dramatic intrusion into their home range. There have been myriad stories of bucks holding tightly while drivers passed by them, yet some whitetailers pooh-pooh such a notion. Apparently, these hunters feel that no deer is a match for their keen eyes and sensitive ears. But if a buck is nervy enough to hold while a pack of hounds— with eyes, ears, *and noses* far keener than ours—bawls at it from three feet away, how much more easily can it escape detection by a hunter? Something to think about the next time you're "pushing bush."

Similarly, the ability of whitetails to adjust their movements—and the timing of them—in response to hunting pressure is something every hunter should be aware of. The work of Simon, Hyngstrom, Root, and Kroll serves as concrete proof that whitetails, constantly aware of disturbances within their home range, can and do make the necessary adjustments to survive most hunting pressure. Being aware of those evasive tactics will make the savvy whitetailer that much more careful when setting up on any deer, particularly a mature buck.

Naturally, you can start some great deer-camp debates over whether deer "know" how to avoid hunting pressure, or if—as some people assume—they simply repeat behaviors that are successful for them until they make a simple mistake or a hunter does something out of the ordinary and kills them. Your take on this matter—and I've heard some pretty heated discussions on the topic—is really not important. What is important is appreciating the whitetail's ability to survive under the intense hunting pressure that occurs across much of its range. Given our superior intellect, top-notch gear, and modern firearms and bows, you'd think the odds of scoring on whitetails would be a lot higher than they are. National success rates, however, tell a far different story.

Perhaps James Kroll summed up this topic best when he quoted longtime friend and whitetail expert Gordon Whittington. Gordon, who's the editor and co-founder of *North American Whitetail* magazine, once told Kroll: "When we make a mistake, we simply lose a deer. When a big buck makes a mistake, he loses his life. There's simply no way we can play the game as seriously as they do."

3

SCOUTING: THE BUILDING BLOCKS FOR SUCCESS

If the deer we remember best are the ones that fool us the worst, the 8-point buck I call Shadow will be burned into my brain forever. I found him completely by accident on a brilliant October afternoon when I took the day off from bowhunting. My excuse for getting out of my treestand that day was Tucker, my pheasant-crazy golden retriever, who put a guilt trip on me as I started gathering my camo for an afternoon in the deer woods. The Minnesota pheasant season was nearly three weeks old, and I'd taken Tucker out only one day. He reminded me of this injustice as I tried to load gear into my truck.

"What are you looking at?" I chided Tuck as he planted himself in my path, whining and wiggling. My wife stood behind our dog as backup.

"He's feeling neglected, I think," Shari said. "We've been hearing that rooster out behind the house the last couple of days."

Now ignoring one overeager pup is well within my abilities, but I was not prepared for a tag team. I sighed and gave Tucker a kiss on the forehead. "So you've been hearin' a cock crow, have you? Well, I guess we can look him up today."

Shari grinned, the dog barked, and I went inside to swap my archery gear for a pumpgun and some brush pants. I had to admit it would feel good to have the ground under my feet for a change, and a little pheasant breast would taste good.

We left right from the house, wading into a tangle of brush and Conservation Reserve Program land (CRP) that grows behind our rural home. It's not a large patch of cover, but it always holds pheasants. And I can hunt it without pestering someone for permission. My good friend Vernon owns it, and he seems downright irritated when I ask, so I don't. Such privilege is always sweet.

I'd already missed one rooster and dumped another when we jumped the buck. He was lying in some tall grass surrounded by a rose bush, and when Tucker nosed into one side of the mess the buck jumped out the other. He flagged at first, then tucked his tail and trotted toward the nearby tree line. He was a perfect 10-point, with a short, heavy rack I'd have been proud to tack on my wall.

"Wow," I mumbled reverently as he minced off. Tucker stared hard after the deer, then got birdy again. In five minutes he'd flushed another rooster, which I scratched down to fill my two-bird limit.

But I wasn't leaving that field without a little detective work. I wandered back to the buck's bed and was fascinated to see the deep, broad impression in the grass. He'd lain there more than once. Following one of three heavy trails leading back to the woods, I quickly found one large rub, then another. A fresh scrape punctuated a trail that angled toward my house.

There were other trails, but I couldn't resist following this path as it wound past a few old apple trees and along some sumac. The buck had several fresh scrapes in the orchard and had cleanly snapped off several wrist-thick sumac stems.

I shook my head as I walked. I'd been chasing bucks on farms as far as thirty miles away and this bruiser was not only traveling behind my house, he was living there. Because he'd been operating under my radar for so long, I nicknamed the buck Shadow.

By the time the dog and I returned home, I'd figured out two trees from which to ambush the buck. Knowing the whitetail wouldn't return that evening, I went out after supper to hang the stands. With only two weeks until the shotgun opener and with the rut about to start, I'd have to move fast to kill this buck. Either breeding urges or hunting pressure would force Shadow from the spot soon.

My discovery was a classic case of too little, too late. Though I saw my monster one time before the gun season began, he was out of range, already following does. And on the opening day of gun season, another hunter beat me to the punch and shot Shadow as the buck crossed a nearby road. Had I discovered this deer earlier, I believe I'd have had an excellent chance of tagging him. I'd simply found him too late in the fall to capitalize on the patterns he'd developed. I was happy for the hunter who bagged Shadow but upset with myself for overlooking such a great deer living right under my nose.

THE NEED FOR SCOUTING

The moral to the above story (other than that I should have taken Tucker pheasant hunting earlier in the season) is, of course, the need for constant scouting. While it's entirely possible to luck into a deer now and then, continual hard-core scouting is the only method that will put you into whitetails on a consistent basis, particularly whitetails adept at avoiding high-pressure areas.

I'm certainly not the first writer to make this claim and I certainly won't be the last, but I'm amazed at the number of hunters who ignore such advice. Whitetail deer are silent, secretive creatures that survive by conducting the majority of their business far from the eyes of hunters. The only way to predict with certainty where deer will appear is to become a master at interpreting their sign. Beds and tracks, rubs and trails, scrapes and droppings—all must be seen, analyzed, and adapted into a carefully constructed hunting plan.

I once asked a local bowhunting expert to break down the percentage of effort he devoted to scouting versus hunting. "I spend a lot of time sitting in treestands every fall," Bob mused. "But those hours are nothing compared to the walking and glassing I do. I'd say over eighty-five percent of my effort is scouting. When I finally decide to sit a particular stand, I want

Hanging stands prior to the hunting season only pays off if you've done a thorough job of scouting. (Pal Reeve photo)

to do so with the confidence that I'm going to shoot a deer there. I hate guessing and I don't trust luck."

While an 85/15 percent breakdown might seem steep to some, the number of trophy-class bucks on my friend's wall serve as proof that his ratios are sound. And I'd argue that any hunter who knowingly pursues pressured deer should scout at least that hard. As the biologists from the previous chapter would remind us, whitetails worried about their survival do not behave like other deer. We will rarely stumble into such deer or find them behaving foolishly. With the possible exception of the rut, when a buck *might* abandon caution to chase does, we are going earn every pressured deer we're fortunate enough to tag.

Now, I realize that the majority of modern deer hunters don't have the time to live in the deer woods, engaging in endless reconnaissance. We live in a time-hungry world, and the hours, days, and weeks of our lives are consumed by myriad factors like family, work, church and/or civic duties, and leisure time. All are legitimate, necessary demands that must be met. Much as we'd like to, we cannot devote our lives to whitetail deer.

But there are few of us who couldn't squeeze in a little more time to become better whitetail hunters. And with a year-round scouting plan, we can spread out our efforts across several months, which will make our study seem less intense and actually offer a more complete picture of the lives of the deer we hunt and the terrain we pursue them in.

Let's take a look at how to develop a methodical, balanced approach to scouting deer that will make the next hunting season our best one.

IN-SEASON AND POST-SEASON SCOUTING

I've only known John Spiegl for a couple of years, but I was impressed by his knowledge of, and devotion to, hunting trophy whitetails right from the start. John has taken mature bucks in several Midwestern states, but he cut his deer-hunting teeth in northern Wisconsin. This region, often called the "Big Woods," is largely forested, lightly populated, and rarely farmed. It is also an area composed mostly of public land. In John's hunting area, land owned by county, state, or federal agencies and timber companies constitutes well over sixty percent of the land base. There are literally hundreds of thousands of acres open to any deer hunter willing to enter this scenic, but often intimidating country.

While John is primarily a bowhunter, he continues to take mature bucks during Wisconsin's annual firearms deer season. He does so by locating areas where deer will flee when pushed by other hunters. John finds these sanctuaries by continually exploring his hunting areas in the off-season.

"When I first started deer hunting, I was like everyone else," John remembers. "I sat in the same spot year after year and just hoped it'd be the right one when the deer started moving. But after a while—usually after you have a bad season—you realize that having just one spot isn't enough. So after one of my bad seasons, I knew I needed to do more looking around."

Naturally, John was looking for deer sign, but he also tried to determine how other hunters were behaving. "Part of it was that I just didn't want to hunt near anyone else," he says. "You put two guys close together and it's not good for either one of them. But I also wanted to know how deer were responding to the pressure. I figured if I knew my area well, and I knew where other guys were going to go, I could find out where the deer would run to escape them. And that's where I wanted to be."

During the deer season, John would note where he saw the vehicles of other hunters. Then, immediately after the season ended, he would revisit these areas to decipher how they were hunting.

"I noticed one pattern almost immediately," he says. "This country contains a lot of low areas like swamps and marshes and creekbeds. Almost all the hunting activity occurred on ground that was high and dry. Whenever those uplands met some water, hunters just stopped."

Realizing that water was a barrier to hunters, John went out of his way to locate spots where water was common. And he soon started locating pockets of almost unhunted deer. "One thing I learned immediately was that water was no barrier to deer," he says. "They'll cross some pretty nasty stuff to escape pressure. Then I found that once the deer had gotten away from hunters they would travel and bed on small areas of dry land. It doesn't take much of a bump in elevation, either; I've seen 'ridges' as low as two or three feet high that deer use all the time."

John's off-season reconnaissance has led him to some fantastic hunting. "Now some of my better spots may be a mile or more away from a road, and water—either a creek or a tag alder swamp or a grassy marsh—prevents most hunters from entering them. If I have to, I'll wear hip boots to walk in. I'll just carry a climbing stand and sling my insulated boots over my shoulder to wear when I get to my spot."

One of John's best areas typifies what he looks for in his post-season scouting trips. "The spot is bordered by a small river and two feeder creeks," he says. "The river is not that wide, but the ground is very wet and marshy on both sides, which makes it difficult to cross. It's all on public land, yet I've never seen anyone in there. We walk in there without spooking deer, mostly by approaching in areas that are wet. Deer aren't afraid to use water if they have to, but they're basically lazy; they're going to stay high and dry if they can. As the season progresses, it seems that there are just more and more deer in there. You can even see them moving around pretty relaxed, even during the gun season."

If you train yourself to look for whitetail habitat where others aren't willing to go, you'll often find good hunting without much competition.

John's reward for finding such a spot has been both satisfying and ongoing; the quiet expert has taken fifteen bucks from the de facto sanctuary within the last decade or so. (Wisconsin allows a hunter to shoot one buck with bow and another with firearms.)

"It's just become an area where the deer seem to know they're safe. Just last year I watched a decent 9-point walk past my stand and toward the uplands about a mile away. He wasn't large enough to shoot, so I just watched him disappear. About an hour and a half later, here he came again, walking back into the swamp. Just like he'd run into those other hunters and decided to get back in."

THE CASE FOR "SPRING" SCOUTING

Perhaps one of the best times to decipher deer patterns and learn new country is during the brief window of time separating winter and summer. Over the years, other whitetail writers and I have referred to this as "spring" scouting, but that's really a misnomer. If you wait for the classic signs of spring—greening leaves and grass, warm temperatures, turkeys strutting—you'll have missed some wonderful scouting opportunities.

Perhaps a better term to describe it would be "off-season" scouting. In northern climes, it typically occurs in a narrow window between snowmelt and green-up. In the South, hunters enjoy a much longer season, as they typically won't have snow to contend with.

Off-season scouting allows a hunter to assemble a much more complete picture of deer movement than he could at any other time of year. In spring and summer, deer sign reveals only current deer patterns, ones that will surely change in the weeks to come. Once hunting seasons arrive, scouting forays must be

Off-season scouting can reveal the trails deer use to reach bedding or feeding areas and escape cover.

Rub lines indicate the presence of bucks and clue you in to where they are headed.

limited and carefully planned; snoop around too much in sensitive spots like bedding areas and other security cover and you risk altering the patterns of the very deer you're trying to hunt.

But once hunters—and somewhat later, snow—have left the woods, a wonderful thing occurs. Last fall's deer sign lies perfectly preserved, waiting to be found and interpreted. Rubs appear almost as fresh as those made in October. Scrapes remain dark and sometimes full of tracks, like they were flash-frozen or held in suspended animation. Trails and crossings and travel corridors lie waiting to be explored. Feel free to bring a buddy or your family, discuss the sign you discover and speculate about good setups for fall. Any deer you spook now will have literally months to forget about your presence.

In many respects, off-season scouting is one of my favorite elements of deer hunting. Not only has it accounted for some awesome stand sites and bucks, it's wonderful exercise, and it has given me a more thorough understanding of how deer use my hunting terrain. I can think of no more satisfying way to spend a late-winter afternoon than traversing the farms and woodlands I visit each fall. Doing so gives me a confidence in my plans for hunting season that I could obtain in no other way.

While I'm convinced that nothing can substitute for a good, thorough walk through a piece of land, I'm blessed in that most of my hunting takes place fairly close to home. This allows me to make multiple visits to these areas. If you're hunting an area that requires some travel and/or your scouting time is severely limited, I'd strongly suggest obtaining a topo map or aerial photos of your ground before you even make the trip. By studying a map or

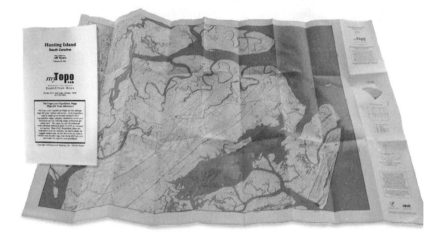

If you don't have year-round access to your hunting grounds, topo maps like this one will help you "scout" from your armchair at home. (MapCard photo)

photo, you can pinpoint high-priority areas to visit during your stay.

Several companies produce computer programs that allow you to download and print topos right from your PC. These programs are excellent tools and I've used them often. One excellent company is Maptech (888-433-8500; www.maptech.com), which has mapped virtually every region in the country. Their user-friendly CDs are, in my opinion, a must-have for any serious deer hunter.

Another innovative product is offered by MapCard (406-259-3134; www.mapcard.com), a company that will print out a topo map or aerial photos of any hunting area you select in the country. These detailed, personalized maps arrive in a few days and can be referred to countless times.

What should you look for when scanning a topo map or aerial photo? Perhaps the most important features are deer-funneling terrain like ridges, benches, and saddles. Regardless of whether an area's "hills" are two thousand feet high or only two feet high, whitetails will use such terrain changes when moving from one piece of cover to the next. Additional funnels include fencelines and similar connecting covers, as well as stream and river corridors and lake edges.

I pay particular attention to all water sources; not only do they serve as barriers to human entry, they also attract whitetails. While the whitetail need for water is well known in arid regions, it is less appreciated in other climates. My experience has shown this to be a great mistake, as deer congregate near water for a variety of reasons: to drink, to browse succulent green plants, and to take advantage of the lush vegetation nearby for security cover.

The final critical element of spring scouting is stand-site preparation. If you intend to hunt from a treestand, there is no better time to prepare your areas than during the off-season. With hunting season months away, you can trim shooting lanes, as well as entry and exit trails, without worrying that your activity will alarm deer. By the time hunting season open, whitetails will have accepted your brush cutting as part of the natural landscape.

Every fall I find that some of my most productive stands are ones I prepped during spring scouting. Situated to take advantage of known travel corridors, and with carefully planned entry and exit routes, I've found that these sites remain productive for many seasons.

SHED ANTLERS—THE KEY TO NEXT YEAR'S BUCK?

Another exciting scouting tool is hunting for shed antlers. Looking for "horns," as most shed-nuts refer to dropped antlers, is gaining popularity among whitetail fanatics, some of whom can barely wait for hunting season to end so they can start gathering bone. At many deer shows, there are contests where sheds are scored on the Boone & Crockett system, and at least one organization (the North American Shed Hunters Club) is entirely devoted to recording the largest sheds among all North American deer species. There are even outfitters who offer hunting adventures for shed antler.

But will finding a buck's sheds help you kill him during the coming season? According to one of my friends, who is among the most hard-core shed hunters I know, the answer is, "It depends." Don Kisky is a southern Iowa farmer and a highly successful whitetailer who, along with his wife Kandi, has tagged over thirty trophy whitetails. Don collects well over a hundred sheds in a typical year, and some of those antlers have keyed him in to deer he's eventually killed.

"Not every shed you find will help you kill a big buck," Don admits. "We have a lot of winter food plots on our farm and on the farms and public wildlife areas where I shed hunt each year. In a tough winter, those food plots will pull bucks in from literally miles around, so sometimes when I find a horn—or set of horns—from a buck, I'm looking at a deer whose home territory might be far away. I'm excited about the find, and it tips me off to the presence of a big buck, but it doesn't necessarily mean I can hunt him that fall."

Shed antler hunting is an enjoyable spingtime activity, and it may pay dividends in the fall.

But sometimes a shed is a vital clue to identifying a buck's core area; the place where he spends most of his time. "Whenever I find an antler near a bedding area or away from a food plot, I really take notice," Don says. "It tells me that I've found a place where the buck feels comfortable, and I immediately ask myself, okay, why is he here? What does he like about this area? Then if I can find some nice rubs or other sign, I might be able to learn a little more about him. Maybe I'll go back and look for him nearby in the summer as he comes to fields in the evening. And if I find the same buck's sheds in the same area for a couple years in a row, I feel like I've really got something."

Don can show you several trophy-class bucks he's killed after finding one or more of their sheds. But one of his most memorable bucks came just a few seasons ago, on a November afternoon when Don was undecided about where to hunt. "The rut had been slow and I was filming with a friend that fall," Don remembers. "I finally said, 'Let's forget the camera, split up, and see if we can make something happen.' I grabbed a bow and a stand, but I had absolutely no idea where I'd sit that night. And then I remembered a little field I'd been ignoring."

The field stuck in Don's mind because that's where he'd found a matched set of antlers from a trophy buck only months before. "And I'd found both of his antlers from the previous year in that same field," he recalls. "Other than one sighting that took place before I'd found those antlers, I had no other information about this deer; no trail monitor photos, no sightings—just two matched sets of horns. For some reason I couldn't get those antlers and that field off my mind, so I went there."

Don Kisky shows off a set of sheds that alerted him to the presence of a nice buck, which he was able to harvest the following season. (Don Kisky photo)

As Don parked his truck at the edge of the field and headed toward the timber, he noticed a big deer ahead of him, crossing the very dirt road he was on. "He was looking right at me, so I froze. When he turned sideways and jumped the fence into that same field, I could see he was a monster buck. As soon as I could move, I dropped my stand and ran toward a big oak tree between the deer and me. I knew the only trail leaving that field passed by that tree. I hadn't waited there five minutes when he showed up, walking straight toward me. When he turned sideways I made the shot. It was the same buck, and his antlers grossed 179 B&C."

For prospective shed hunters who are having trouble finding antlers, Don offers the following advice. "Random walking is no good," he stresses. "I grid-pattern certain sections and walk them systematically. If I'm walking a hill, for example, I'll start ten yards from the bottom and walk around the entire hill at that level. Then I move up a ways and do the same thing, continuing up the hill until I've covered it all. I want to find every antler in the area."

Don recommends that hunters carry binoculars to identify parts of antlers. "I tell myself I'm looking for a small, dark-brown tine laying on dark-brown leaves," he laughs. "And I walk slow. The binoculars let me check out something from fifty yards away without walking over to pick it up. That can save you literally miles of walking in a day. And I've found that timing is everything. It's easy to get too excited and rush into an area while bucks are still carrying. In a cold winter in my area, bucks will shed earlier, but on a yearly average, I'd say the peak times are in late February to mid-March."

When Don finds an antler, he writes down the date and location on the antler beam in pencil. "That way, I never forget where and when I find a horn, and I can tell patterns when I find a couple from the same buck a couple of years in a row."

The quiet, slow-paced work of the shed hunter might seem light-years away from the frenetic pace of fall hunting season. But if finding the "horns" of a good buck provides one more piece of the puzzle about whitetail behavior in a hunting area, those miles of walking will be worth every step.

High-tech hunters can note the presence of buck sightings, rubs, scrapes, and trails, plug the coordinates into a GPS, and then use the information to establish patterns.

SCOUTING IN THE SALAD DAYS:
SUMMER AND EARLY FALL

As a young whitetailer, summer seemed interminable to me. Long weeks of searing heat and humidity made deer season seem like a distant dream. Outside of shooting my bow and readying gear, I could think of nothing to do but wait, wait, and wait some more.

These days, I know that summer can be one of the best times to census buck populations in a hunting area. In fact, there may be no time of year when bucks are as highly visible as in summer, particularly in farm country, where whitetails take advantage of lush food sources like alfalfa, soybeans, and other succulent crops. But even in more forested areas, whitetails can frequently be seen moving in and around openings, feeding on grasses and sedges. During summer, nutrition is a priority for all whitetails; does need high-quality feed to nurse hungry fawns, and bucks are pouring on calories to boost antler growth and body weight. This "need for feed" frequently makes deer move in the open and often well before dark.

Observing an active field or feeding zone can be an eye-opening experience. Bucks are still in bachelor groups ranging from two to a dozen or more animals. While many of these bucks will disperse as fall begins, some will remain faithful to the general area. That makes getting a first glance at the area's animals an important part of the scouting process.

I've known many hunters who were able to spot a buck in summer, then harvest him later in the fall. These bucks were either killed as they remained in a summer pattern near where they were first observed or shot some distance away after the hunter used his spring scouting information to discover the buck's fall home.

To observe summer deer, first determine their preferred forage. Often an evening drive will reveal the current choice of foods. Lush alfalfa and clover are attractive throughout summer, especially just prior to cutting. Soybeans are a hot ticket, as long as they remain green and flowering. As soon as the plant begins to turn brown, the palatability gradually diminishes for deer.

Once you locate an active field, set up on the far side of it, downwind from anticipated entry points. Bring a powerful set of binoculars or a spotting scope so you don't have to set up too close to feeding whitetails. It's important not to spook animals when you leave. If you can climb a small knoll or other observation point so much the better. I've hidden in the first rows of a cornfield or slipped inside an abandoned farm building so that my scent and silhouette remain hidden from deer. I can sneak quietly away when darkness falls.

As you observe animals, note their entry points into the field and the approximate time they use them. If you're lucky enough to be able to hunt during an early bow or muzzleloader season, the patterns you observe might still be in place when your season opens. But even if you can't hunt these deer until well into the fall, gaining such a census of buck populations and sizes will be valuable. Though bachelor groups will disperse and territories change, using the knowledge you gained during spring and summer scouting could help you locate one of the bucks you see.

Summer observation is a valuable and exciting tool.

SPY GAMES:
USING REMOTE CAMERAS TO DISCOVER DEER

They haven't been on the market very many years, but motion-sensing cameras are quickly changing the way many hunters scout. These cameras, which emit an infrared light beam that triggers the camera's shutter, can be placed in an area of high deer traffic to snap candid photos of whitetails. Housed in a tough, weatherproof shell that straps onto a tree or fencepost, remote cameras can literally scout while you sleep. There may be no more effective tool for discovering a secretive buck's presence than a motion camera.

My friend Ron Bice agrees. As an employee of Wildlife Research Center, Inc., Ron has been using motion cameras for several seasons. He has taken some of the most stunning (often daylight) images of trophy whitetails that I've ever seen. My personal experience with cameras has been limited, so I picked Ron's brain about the best way to capture images like his.

"I guess my first, best exposure to motion cameras was when I started using them on a property I hunt," Ron says. "I'd been hearing people talk about a giant buck they'd seen off and on for the last couple of years. Since they were non-hunters, I took their descriptions of his rack with a grain of salt. Even an experienced hunter can get over-excited about good antlers, and if this buck was as good as they said he was, he was far bigger than anything I'd seen there."

Nevertheless, Ron put out a camera overlooking a mock scrape, and before long he'd captured the buck. "He was every bit as large as people said he was," Ron enthused. "Ten perfect, typical points, long main beams . . . he would easily net 170. I was

Remote-sensing cameras have been a boon to whitetail hunters. (Pat Reeve photo)

amazed. I haven't been able to harvest him yet, but you have no idea what a motivator that picture was for me. On those mornings when I don't feel like hunting, it gets me out of bed."

Ron has set cameras in a variety of locations, but experience has shown him that artificial, or mock, scrapes produce the best images. "My first step, before I ever leave the house, is to take a scent-reducing shower. [Wildlife Research soaps are ideal for this.] Probably one of the most overlooked steps in getting good photos is to be as clean as possible. I wear rubber boots and gloves to aid in this process—from the time I leave the vehicle until I return.

"Then I head to an area where I believe there'll be a good possibility of buck travel. In late summer it can be a field where you've seen bachelor groups. After velvet shed, I look for trails leading out of bedding areas. Once I've found a good spot, I look for a tree that's typical of a species deer would scrape underneath in that area. It should have an overhanging branch that's about five feet high or so. If it doesn't, you can cut your own and tie it to the tree with cord.

"Then I make a mock scrape on the ground, using a shed antler to scrape away leaves and vegetation. On the overhanging branch I hang either a Scent Wick or Ultimate Scrape Dripper with the appropriate scent on it. Early in the season an attracting lure like Trail's End #307 works very well. Closer to the rut, I'll use either a territorial scent like Mega-Tarsal Plus or an estrous scent like Special Golden Estrous.

"Mount the camera on a tree, keeping it slightly lower than your scent dispenser and framed so the dispenser is in the middle of the shot. This will give you the best view of the antlers when the buck comes in to the setup. I want the camera about seven feet off the trail, which gives me a good close-up shot of the buck when he comes in."

Ron's final step is, in his mind, the reason he's been so successful at capturing high-quality images. "Once I'm ready to leave, I spray down everything I've touched with Scent Eliminator spray—leaves, trees, branches. Then, I walk out backward for about the first ten or fifteen yards, spraying the ground in front of me as I walk. I can't stress enough eliminating, or at least significantly reducing, human scent during this process. We simply

This camera caught a group of bachelor bucks lined up to take a sniff at a mock scrape. Images like this help hunters zero in on productive hunting areas. (Wildlife Research Center, Inc. photo)

can't underestimate the power of the whitetail nose, and I don't want the buck feeling alarmed around this site at all. While we can never totally eliminate our scent, taking these precautions will leave little evidence that I've lingered in this spot for any length of time."

Ron also stresses multiple camera setups. "I believe that most mature bucks will react to the camera flash," he says. "It won't startle them enough to cause them to abandon the area, of course, but for some of the spookier deer, it may be a couple of days before they return. I see this all the time in my setups. I may shoot nine or ten really nice pictures the first day I set a camera, then nothing for three or four days. So now I pull a camera immediately after the first setup, then move it to a new location."

Will snapping a buck's candid photo lead you directly to a close encounter or a kill? Perhaps not. But it will, as in the case of Ron's monster 10-point, tip you off to the presence of a deer you never knew existed.

Like shed hunting, remote camera pictures represent a small but important glimpse into the mysterious life of a big buck. Combine this information with other data you've assembled—off-season rub lines and scrapes, deer behavior observed in hunting season, shed antlers, or late summer observations—and you could piece together a clearer picture of the buck, with you in the same frame. In the world of whitetail hunting, there's rarely such a thing as too much information.

FINAL THOUGHTS

Performing all the scouting practices described in this chapter might seem like an exhaustive, time-consuming task. They can be, and many experts are happy to admit it. However, when spread out in small chunks of effort across an entire year, they become much easier to accomplish. For the price of a couple of hours a week, your knowledge of deer behavior in your area, as well as your ability to identify the presence of any mature bucks, will increase exponentially.

Assuming that you stick to the same basic hunting grounds each year, you can multiply that knowledge many times over as the seasons pass. If you can learn one significant thing every year about your hunting land and the whitetails that inhabit it, you'll find yourself hunting far more effectively and efficiently than ever before, even when matched against cagey, hard-hunted bucks.

STAND-HUNTING TACTICS

Sometimes the shots you *don't* take are the ones that haunt you. There were twenty-three minutes left of opening day of the firearms season, and I was staring at what was then the largest 8-point whitetail buck I'd ever seen. He had a face as black as an Angus steer's, which made his ivory antlers appear spectral, like a tall, spreading halo. And the doe he was following? Well, she'd just minced daintily down the trail, twenty-five steps from my tree and fully broadside.

Of course, I counted on the buck following her. I had even shifted my feet to point to the opening she had just walked through. And then the buck just stopped and stared at me. I had been around big whitetails enough to know that the stop-and-stare was something they pulled all the time, on principle if for no other reason. But I still fought a small, dull panic. Minus some quivering, which was mostly internal and totally quiet, I was solid as a post. My stand was squeezed between a white pine and a red oak, and to that buck I had to look like nothing more than a snow-covered branch. So there was nothing to do but wait.

Lots of things go through your mind when a trophy buck is eyeballing you. Mostly I prayed he wouldn't see my nose dripping or the little vapors of breath that escaped the corners of my mouth. I have long believed that whitetails sense it if you look at them too long, so I averted my gaze to a clump of brush just to the left of the buck. But I couldn't keep this up forever, and when my eyes shifted back to him I noticed a small but clear path for my bullet that led right to the base of his neck. He was facing me dead-on, and though I normally wait for a broadside shot, I knew if I hit the buck at this spot he would drop; if not instantly, then within a few yards of feeling the slug from my muzzleloader.

So I forgot the nose drips and my frozen breath and started a little argument in my head. I'm paraphrasing, but the first voice said something like, "The buck is sixty yards, tops. It's a cake shot. Raise the gun slowly, draw a bead, and put the bullet in his goodie box."

"What?" screamed Voice Two. "You move that barrel now and that gosh-awful monster is gonna trip on himself flushing out of here. You saw what the doe did. Once he relaxes he'll follow her, and you can kill him with a stick if you want to."

"Remember those deer you muffed because you waited for the perfect shot instead of taking the first good one?" Voice One taunted. "Does the word 'replay' mean anything to you? Be aggressive for once in your life."

"Do *not* listen to Mr. Snap Shot, pleeeeaaase," said Voice Two. "You pride yourself on patience and clean, one-shot kills. Let this play out, and you'll tag this buck. Then we can go home and get warm."

Just then the buck flicked his tail, dropped his head, and started down the trail toward the doe. When his rack disappeared behind a young white pine I raised the barrel and settled the bead on the next opening. The buck had to take no more than five steps to reach that wide, wonderful, slam-dunk gap. Voice Two was just about to say "I told you so" when a long, loud whistle sounded from a nearby ridge.

The buck stopped. There was a second whistle, and the doe—who'd been browsing contentedly for the duration—nervously stomped her foot. It took a second for it to register, but suddenly I knew the whistler was my father, whom I'd heard shoot a deer about midafternoon. He must be signaling for help with the dragging. But why now? Couldn't he wait until dark, when a black-faced buck wearing a beautiful halo would be lying dead at his son's feet?

"Of course he couldn't!" screamed Voice One. "And there goes your buck!" My once-relaxed monster had not blown out in a hasty escape; he had simply taken two steps backward, turning slowly and slinking like a rabbit through the brush. I had no shot for several seconds, but as the buck topped a small ridge that would hide him from me forever, I spotted a small opening. I swung the gun, saw hide beyond the muzzle, and pulled the trigger. The buck disappeared.

My heart sank as I crawled down the tree steps. Naturally, I prayed that the buck lay on the other side of the ridge. But I am not a matchless shot. I have killed the vast majority of my deer by waiting for sure opportunities, and the one I'd just seized was as tough as I'd ever taken. Still, I remained hopeful as I scanned the leaves for blood; perhaps I'd pulled this off and would recover the trophy. But just as I'd resolved to stop my search until I had help, I heard three quick shots echo from a nearby ridgeline. Later that evening I would learn not only that I'd missed the buck, but that he'd put the burners on and sprinted some four hundred yards, coming to a stop only twenty yards from our neighbor, who had killed "my" buck and claimed the biggest whitetail of his life.

Naturally, I was heartsick about losing out on such a terrific whitetail (and, I should add, very proud and pleased for our neighbor, who's a fine friend and sportsman), but Time has been a good healer. Now I recognize that hunt as solid proof that while Luck may not have smiled on me, my technique was as sound as they come. I'd chosen to sit in a treestand on the gun-hunting opener and let other hunters push deer to me.

Over the years I've come to believe this is among the most effective methods for consistently tagging pressured whitetails.

THE CASE FOR STAND HUNTING

The logic, of course, is hard to refute. Waiting for deer to come to you is a proven technique practiced by scores of hunters. Pressured deer are frequently on the move, goaded from their beds by the presence of hunters. To let those hunters work for you—in essence, push deer while you wait—seems one of the most logical methods a hunter can employ. Sneaking up on a whitetail is difficult business at best; driving them can be like pushing Jell-O through a straw. So why not stay put and let deer come to you?

Stand hunting is a great way to intercept whitetails that have been put on the move by other hunters in the area.

There are other advantages. Stand hunting allows a hunter to remain largely silent and motionless, thereby defeating the sharp eyes and keen ears of whitetails. The tactic is also among the most effective at minimizing human scent, provided winds are consistent. This helps us win the battle against the whitetail's nose. The stand hunter, especially if he's using an elevated platform, can often spot deer much more readily than hunters using other methods. Greater shooting accuracy is also a possibility for the stand hunter, as he's frequently shooting at a relaxed whitetail that's unaware of his presence.

Safety is an added, though no less important, benefit for the stand hunter. He remains in one spot and, assuming he's wearing quality safety gear and obeying sound gun-handling rules, will be more visible to other hunters and less likely to engage in risky behavior or take shots that could result in an accident.

Finally, the argument could be made that, in some situations at least, hunting from a stand or blind is the most ethical method as it results in less interference with other sportsmen.

A DIFFERENT MINDSET

But there is a difference between applying this method to pressured deer and using it to ambush whitetails moving in traditional patterns (from bed to feed and back again or during the rut or even as a means for calling and rattling). Stand hunting for pressured whitetails requires an understanding of deer behavior that anticipates where animals will head when pushed and the knowledge that sometimes these places will differ from normal bedding cover.

Stand hunting for pressured deer also means making adjustments for deer that may not move at the often predictable hours used by most feeding whitetails. While the hunter seeking non-pressured deer can make a qualified guess that deer will be active at dawn or dusk, pressured deer may arrive at literally any time of day. I've sat in stands for the first three hours of daylight and barely seen a deer, only to be surrounded by whitetails at high noon.

The buck described in the beginning of this chapter arrived well after 4 PM and was only the fourth whitetail I'd seen all day. Sure he was worth the wait, but I'd be lying if I didn't admit that there were some long, long hours separating deer sightings. Indeed, there have been days—as shots rang out around me and I imagined every hunter in the area tagging out but me—when I spent hours wondering if my stand was in the wrong spot. But in most cases, hanging in there proved worthwhile.

Stand hunters must have great patience to wait out a nice buck like this one. (Pat Reeve photo)

So patience, that quality so easy to discuss and so hard to adopt, is the key to effective stand hunting. But patience is worth little if you're waiting in the wrong place. Just as whitetails do in every situation, pressured deer seek out specific terrain and cover types, and only those stands placed in the areas with the highest odds will produce consistently.

Let's take a look at some of those areas.

TRAVEL ROUTES:
TAKING DEER ON THE MOVE

Most hunters know that pressured deer seek security cover: dense stands of trees and/or brush, bedding areas where they can readily detect danger, and pockets of cover that people rarely invade. Hunting in such covers can be effective, but also difficult. An alternate strategy is to ambush deer on their way to these havens by setting up on a travel route.

We know that pressured deer often increase the amount and frequency of their travel until they find a safe haven. But to find such cover they usually use travel routes that will lead them to security in the fastest, most discreet way. While this seems an obvious point, it's an important one because it means there are many (sometimes quite obvious) trails that a pressured whitetail will probably *not* use. For example, the well-worn path leading to a lush alfalfa field that served a bowhunter well in September may be devoid of whitetails when that same hunter is sharing the woods with an army of orange-clad brethren.

Similarly, other feeding-type trails that meander through mature timber, low grasslands, and other open areas will seldom—except in extreme situations—be used by pressured whitetails. I mention this only because of the large number of deer hunters I've seen set up on such runways, blindly hoping that a buck will trot by.

So what travel routes will whitetails use when seeking deep cover? Generally, they are paths that allow deer to reach a secure area quickly without exposing themselves. It's important to remember that whitetails, provided they have not been forced from their home range, intimately know the places where they feel safe and several paths to get there. Take, for example, a buck that has a preferred bedding area on the end of a long ridge. There may be a half dozen trails leading to this safe haven, but only one or two that the buck will use in daylight hours or when he feels threatened. Only scouting and experience will reveal those paths.

I once hunted a massive buck that used such a bedding area. During my off-season scouting I located a small, pool-table-sized plateau on the end of a bluff that was matted with stiff, gray deer hair, indicating a well-used bed. The trees ringing this plateau were raked with huge rubs. On the open-timbered ridgetop, I found a path the size of a cow track beaten to that bed. I set up on this trail three times during the archery season and saw the buck once, but just as he approached bow range, a nearby doe distracted him.

The following spring I intensified my scouting, knowing the buck had to have another route to his haven. While clambering over the sidehills I discovered not one, but two more trails. One snaked through a dense blackberry thicket on the east side of the hill, the other slid among thick white cedars to the west. Each trail would have easily allowed the buck to reach his bed completely undetected while I sat in my ridgetop stand only one hundred yards away. After eating my plate of humble pie, I went to work and brushed out a stand site on each of these trails. I was sure my discovery and hard work would put this deer on my wall that fall.

But Fate can be a cruel. Vowing to stay off my new routes until I had the perfect wind direction, I waited through much of the season to snap my trap. But as I visited the farm for an afternoon hunt, the farmer pulled me aside. "This deer look familiar?" he asked, pointing to a monstrous rack on the floor of his shed. It was my buck.

"Where'd you get that?" I mumbled incredulously.

"Found him in the ditch yesterday," my friend replied. "Sawed the rack off so you could see it. He musta been hit by a car."

I don't know how they do it, but even in death big bucks can cheat you.

Still, I felt good about working hard to figure out a difficult deer and learning some valuable lessons in the process. The ridgetop trail I'd watched was a viable setup, but it was only one path the buck took to sanctuary. The other trails, which kept the buck hidden in dense cover and beneath the slope, were probably much preferred. In the many seasons since that fall, I've kept a sharp eye out for similar subtle routes, and they usually produce.

Some classic travel routes used by pressured deer include benches and saddles in hilly country. In farm or prairie terrain, an overgrown fencerow, a brush- or weed-choked ditch, and a tree-lined creek or river bottom are prime examples. Hunters in heavily timbered country will find whitetails following lakeshores, dry ridges in a swamp, or the edges of clearcuts or lines of brush through otherwise open timber.

If possible, always scout thoroughly before you hang stands. Knowing that you are set up on a fresh, well-used travel corridor will boost your confidence.

Again, the scouting methods discussed in the preceding chapter will help identify such travel routes. After extensive walking has revealed security covers in your area, take the time to mark them on topo maps and aerial photos. Then take a long, hard look at these references to determine the travel corridors deer are likely to take to reach them.

You can make even more sophisticated guesses about which corridors will receive the most use if you know the areas that receive the most pressure from other hunters. One of the most exciting things about discovering such areas is that they will frequently produce for many seasons. Unless there is a major land use or vegetation change (a CRP field is put back into production or a once-brushy area grows into mature timber), whitetails will use these travel corridors year after year.

WHEN LESS IS MORE: ESTABLISHING SANCTUARIES

If your scouting and hunting efforts have revealed some whitetail security covers, it's tempting to set up right in the midst of these havens. I've done just that and managed to see and/or harvest some fine deer. But I can say from experience that this practice can be as risky as it is successful. Anytime you invade security cover, you run the risk of being detected by deer and affecting their continued use of the area. Whitetails, especially mature bucks, will quickly abandon even a preferred bedding cover— and likely not return to it for several days—after they've been "bumped."

This knowledge has led to the rather cutting-edge practice known as "establishing sanctuaries." Simply put, this means identifying one or more security covers in your area and vowing to stay out of them, no matter the number or quality of whitetails they might hold. By giving deer such undisturbed islands of cover, you stand a greater chance of keeping deer within the confines of your property instead of flushing them out and exposing them to potential harvest by other hunters.

I know two groups of highly successful hunters who employ this tactic. The first is the father/son team of Neil and Craig Dougherty, who own and manage five hundred acres of whitetail habitat in Steuben County, New York. The Doughertys have spent a decade carving a whitetail paradise out of this forested hill country, establishing food plots and managing their timber for maximum wildlife habitat. By limiting the harvest of young bucks and killing a significant percentage of does each fall, they've created a quality hunting ground from an area that once had very limited potential. One crucial management strategy has been identifying and establishing sanctuaries where there is absolutely no human trespass allowed during the hunting season.

According to Neil, sanctuaries don't have to be large in order to be successful. "We have several on our five hundred acres," he says. "Two are about fifteen acres in size, but we have a couple of smaller ones that may only be three to five acres. That's plenty big enough to hold a mature buck. We locate ours well away from property borders. This insures us that hunters from neighboring properties won't trespass into them or hunt their edges. We want deer to feel safe once they reach sanctuaries, and they do. And we want the sanctuaries to be there every year, because deer intimately know the areas where they can go and not be disturbed. By using the same spots year after year, you're 'teaching' generations of does and their offspring where they are."

Neil notes that the best sanctuaries are areas of thick cover or rugged terrain. "An excellent place to establish a sanctuary is in an area that's already difficult to hunt," he says. "If steep hillsides or topography result in swirling winds or other tough hunting conditions, why not just let the place alone and let it work for you? If deer want to retreat to these places, let them. They'll spend more time on your property and feel safer. Then when they do move, you'll stand a much better chance of harvesting them."

The Doughertys have had tremendous success with this approach, but perhaps none more memorable than the fall of 2002, when Craig took a whopper buck. "I was watching a food plot during the late muzzleloader season, which occurs after our general firearms and archery season," Craig recalls. "My stand overlooked one of our food plots, which held several does. The deer were feeding heavily on brassicas we'd planted. Those plants become attractive to deer in late fall and early winter, and this was early winter, with plenty of snow and cold.

"Suddenly I looked up and there was a tremendous buck entering the food plot. After joining the does and feeding for a while, the buck finally turned broadside and gave me a 125-yard shot. I knew that was within range of the muzzleloader, and I was fortunate to make a good shot on him."

After celebrating Craig's tremendous, wide-racked 10-point, Neil immediately decided to learn something about the buck. "Since there was fresh snow on the ground, I backtracked the deer to see where he'd been bedding prior to entering the food plot," Neil says. "I wasn't surprised when I found his trail leading directly to one of the small sanctuaries we'd established. I'm

This hunter is examining an escape trail that leads to security cover. Successful stand hunters learn to take advantage of these travel routes. (Pat Reeve photo)

firmly convinced that buck had spent a good deal of the season bedding in that little pocket of cover."

The Doughertys aren't the only hunters who've used the sanctuary concept to score on heavily hunted whitetails. Kevin Small is a northern Missouri whitetail guide who's been employing the technique for several seasons. "Basically, I decided to try it on a chunk of ground where I spooked deer every time I took a hunter in there," Kevin laughs. "I just got tired of bumping them and screwing things up. I knew there were some nice bucks living on this farm, so I thought, 'What the heck, let's just stay out of there and let them have it.' I kept an eye on this area, and once our rifle season started the deer just piled in there. Then the light bulb really came on for me. I thought, 'Why not try this on other farms I hunt?'"

Kevin did just that, and has found that creating sanctuaries has improved his success rates on both attracting and harvesting deer. "It just results in deer that are more relaxed and continue to move well," he stresses. "You're able to hunt the farm, and you're just not tipping your hand every time you do. It's kind of ironic, but sometimes the best way to hunt a deer is to leave him alone. If you get aggressive with a mature buck—and that's a trap that's easy to fall into—it's pretty easy to lose."

Kevin's experience has led him to adopt some general principles for not only creating sanctuaries, but also hunting the areas around them.

Here are his tips:

- Escape cover is relatively dense, but also contains easy entry and exit routes that deer can follow. Deer feel safest when they can see, smell, and avoid danger.

- The best sanctuaries are places you have difficulty hunting anyway; you'll be less tempted to invade them.
- If you can, plant small food plots fairly close to the sanctuary so you'll have an attractant that will draw deer from the protected area to a setup of your choosing.
- Hunting the borders or edges of a sanctuary is fine, but never do so if the wind direction is blowing into the sanctuary. Also, plan entry and exit routes to your stand sites that won't disturb deer in the sanctuary. Clip or mow paths for silent walking, or follow a creekbed or ditch that will hide your noise and silhouette.

The experiences of hunters like the Doughertys and Kevin Small highlight one of deer hunting's great conundrums: Backing off on a deer can sometimes be the key to killing him. We're all tempted to rush in and hunt some hot spot we've found, but in many cases such aggressive tactics hurt, rather than help, our chances. As Kevin Small says, "I've located those buck bedding areas and hunted them. I've also ruined a lot of great areas by doing that. In my book, when you make an aggressive move on a mature deer like that, you're limiting yourself to one chance to kill him. After that, he's probably on to you and things just got a whole lot tougher. I'd rather back off and let him make a mistake."

GOING FOR BROKE

Of course, many deer hunters do not own land or don't have the luxury of managing the ground they hunt. Or they hunt public areas where doing so is impossible, and maybe illegal. In such situations, hunting security cover such as bedding areas is an option. As I mentioned earlier, I've hunted such areas in the past and have experienced some good action. The problem is that it's frequently short-lived; once resident deer know you've invaded their safe places, they either abandon them or become very adept at avoiding you.

But if you're forced to swing for the bleachers, you can have success if you hunt carefully. For starters, try to identify as many bedding areas or security covers as possible. This will allow you to spread your efforts among several areas instead of hunting just one spot and burning it out. Before the hunt, determine the right wind directions for hunting each area and pledge not to hunt there if conditions aren't ideal. Some hunters I know keep a printed log or journal of their stand sites and the best winds for hunting each area. Such a log is a good reminder if you're stumped about where to go on a particular day.

Spend as much time selecting entry and exit routes as you do stand sites. Getting into, and back out of, security covers without alerting deer is one of the most challenging elements of hunting them. I like to clip a small trail into densely wooded sites so I can sneak in and out without stepping on twigs or brushing against tree limbs that might alert nearby whitetails. If you can follow a path that hides your silhouette, such as a creekbed, ditch, or the backside of a ridge, so much the better.

One of the slickest approaches to a treestand that I use involves canoeing up a long creek to a riverbottom island. I can beach my canoe within a hundred yards of my stand and slip in to my spot within minutes of leaving the boat. The approach is completely silent and, of course, leaves no scent trail.

Once you've located a good stand site, clear shooting lanes well before the start of the season so any whitetails in the area have time to get used to the changes.

If possible, prepare your stand sites before the season. Invariably, it will be necessary to trim some branches in order to shoot through the thick cover. (I do this as sparingly as possible in bedding areas; mature bucks seem to sense when they've entered a "hole" in otherwise dense vegetation.) If it's legal, I may leave a portable treestand in the spot. If not, I prepare the stand tree and bring a lightweight stand with me the morning of the hunt. If you plan to hunt from the ground, erecting a blind made of natural materials long before the season will give whitetails time to accept it as part of the landscape.

Finally, when you hunt such a spot, get there long before dawn and stay there all day. (Unless you tag a deer, of course!) You want to arrive before whitetails start entering the area in the morning, and if you try to sneak out after a couple of hours or to grab some lunch, you'll be spooking any deer that have arrived to bed down. This will burn out an area just as quickly as firing shots and talking.

It's been my experience that pressured whitetails arrive at security cover throughout the day. Remember, some of these animals may be coming from a long distance to reach the spot, and it can take them some time to maneuver through a gauntlet of other hunters. Also, whitetails that have bedded in other areas will get bumped as hunters tire of stand hunting (or get cold), break for lunch, or gather to make drives.

There's no question that sticking in a stand for eight to ten hours a day can be a tiresome, often boring vigil. But to hunt a bedding area in any other fashion is simply not doing the spot justice. If you've gone to the trouble of locating and setting up in such a key area, take an extra dose of patience pills and let that setup work for you.

While there are many stands on the market these days, portable stands usually provide hunters with the most versatility. (Pat Reeve photo)

GEAR AND SAFETY CONSIDERATIONS FOR THE STAND HUNTER

I admit that I live a somewhat tortured existence when it comes to hunting gear. I cherish simplicity and traveling light, yet I also adore quality gear and love nothing more than testing out new toys. As my wife and kids will attest, my closets overflow with hunting gear, some of which is used over and over, some of which I just don't have the heart to throw away.

Confessions aside, quality gear can make or break any sportsman, but stand hunters have their own special needs. For starters, the very practice requires an extra piece of gear other methods do not—the stand itself. I've been hunting from treestands for some twenty-six years now, and I've become pretty finicky about what I hunt from. I appreciate a bargain as much as anyone, but when it comes to treestands, I'll pay a few extra dollars for higher quality. Remember, the main function of an elevated platform is not to help you kill a deer, it's to keep you safely aloft so you can crawl back down the tree and join friends and loved ones at the end of the day.

There are many options for hunters who want to "get elevated" while they wait for deer. My personal preference is portable, hang-on type stands, which appeal to me because the good ones are light, easy to transport and hang, silent, and cause little or no damage to a tree. I use them in conjunction with tree steps or climbing sticks, which are also sturdy, silent, and easy to use. These features allow me to erect a stand and then "pull it" at the end of the day's hunt or leave it in place for another day. This setup is also the most versatile in my book, as you can adapt it to virtually any size and/or shape of tree capable of holding a stand.

Portable ladder steps allow hunters to set up without damaging stand trees.

There are, naturally, many other treestand options. Today's climbing stands are light years better than the original models, and I know several outstanding hunters who swear by them. The only drawback to climbers is the need to find a limbless tree, which is difficult in some hunting areas. Some of the climber fans I know identify stand trees as they scout, and if there are too many limbs, they simply prune them preseason to "prepare" them for the hunting season.

Ladder stands are a recent innovation and provide wonderful stability and ease of use. While they look ungainly and seem easy for deer to spot, my friends who've used them don't report getting busted any more frequently than they do in portables. In fact, I shot a muzzleloader buck two seasons ago from a ladder stand, and the dark-horned 8-point walked to within bow range and never knew I was there. The only disadvantage of ladder stands is the weight and bulk, which require that they be set up preseason. And, of course, moving them is more difficult than it is with other models, which robs you of mobility and the chance to fine-tune your hunting location.

I'll probably ruffle some feathers here, but I am not a fan of permanent stands. Part of this prejudice stems from my belief that deer—especially those being hunted with some intensity—learn where most of these ambush spots are situated and avoid them. This simply makes permanent stands less effective.

My second prejudice concerns respect and aesthetics. If you own land and want to erect a permanent setup that is your right. But I hunt land that is owned by others—either private landowners or county, state, and federal governments—and I believe it's wrong (and, of course, in some cases just plain illegal) to permanently alter woodlands that don't belong to me.

I've had more than one landowner complain to me about previous hunters who'd damaged trees by pounding spikes and nails into potentially valuable timber. Not only do these property owners begrudge the financial loss of such damage, they often regard the stand as a visual blight on the landscape. My personal ethic is to leave as little evidence of my presence as possible. Even the flimsiest, cobbled-together platform will remain for many years after a hunter erects it.

Finally, but of no less importance, I dislike "permanent" stands because they can be hazardous. Even a once-sturdy construction project can weaken or rot as the wind and elements work on it between deer seasons. You don't have to read many accident reports to find tales of hunters who tumbled from their "trusty" old stands as a step gave way or a platform disintegrated beneath their feet. Most of these accidents could be avoided if the hunter had invested in a quality, factory-made stand instead of relying on a homemade death trap.

As long as I'm preaching safety let me stress the need for a quality safety harness regardless of the elevated platform you choose. Every fall, dozens of hunters take nasty falls—some resulting in permanent injury or even death—that could have been prevented by a safety harness. There are many quality models on the market, but I suggest two important requirements when selecting a harness. First, it should hold you upright in case of a fall and not restrict your breathing. Second, it should be easy to wear and comfortable; this means that wearing the thing is not a chore, so you'll employ it as just another part of your gear. The most expensive harness on the market is worthless if you leave it sitting in the truck because it's too cumbersome to put on.

Of course, you don't need to climb a tree in order to kill deer, and ground blinds are certainly a viable (and in some situations, the only) option. Hunters were tagging whitetails from ground blinds long before the boom of the commercially made treestand. A well-constructed blind made of natural materials can be deadly on whitetails. Again, for maximum effectiveness, these hides should be constructed long before the season and hunted only when the wind is right. Whitetails are amazingly adept at spotting even a carefully camouflaged blind, but given time they'll often accept it as part of the landscape.

Some of the manufactured portable ground blinds that have recently become available offer an exciting alternative to cutting brush and constructing a blind. Many of these are reasonably lightweight, and all of the best models can be erected in seconds. This gives the ground-blind hunter an option of portability that was previously impossible.

Another exciting feature of these blinds is that they help to contain human scent, which allows hunters a greater array of choices when setting up. I've used these blinds extensively for turkey hunting, and they're wonderful tools. My friends who employ them for whitetails say they can be equally deadly on deer, though much more effective if erected, brushed in, and allowed to "sit" for a day or two.

Since stand hunting is a practice that often puts you in close contact with deer, silence is a quality I insist on for all clothing and additional gear. For undergarments, I prefer light cotton in early season and polypropylene and/or fleece as the weather turns cold. In the past, finding quality outerwear (especially rough-weather garments) was a real challenge, but these

Hunting success depends more on knowing how and when whitetails use an area than on whether you choose a treestand or ground blind.

days there are a number of companies making warm, dry, silent clothing that is just wonderful. It may take some extra money to purchase this quality clothing, but it will prove its worth on the first lousy-weather hunt you endure.

Another important piece of my clothing ensemble is a roomy daypack. I've learned that layering clothing is the way to achieve comfort while stand hunting, and my daypack serves as a de facto clothes drawer. I'll wear the bare minimum on my walk to a stand site, then don additional clothing once I settle in. In the main compartment of the pack I may carry rain/snow gear, a fleece vest or extra shirt, hats (up to three stocking or balaclava-style hats, depending on the weather), and gloves and mittens. Strapped to the outside of the pack will be any seriously bulky items like insulated jackets or bibs.

The daypack totes other essential gear, such as binoculars, deer calls, tree steps, deer drag, matches and fire starter, and a cell phone if I'm hunting alone. I'm also a nut about carrying food and liquid, especially in cold weather. Your body burns a lot of calories staying warm, and I find I hunt much longer and more effectively if I keep my furnace fueled with high-carbohydrate and fatty foods, and drink plenty of water.

FINAL THOUGHTS

The stand hunter might seem like a passive type, waiting with seemingly blind faith for a whitetail to pass by his little place in the woods. But the best stand hunters I know are anything but passive and never blind. They scout aggressively to determine whitetail behavior and identify preferred covers. They do their best to understand the patterns and behaviors of other hunters and how these affect deer. And they use patience—perhaps one of our society's most endangered qualities—to get within effective range of one of Nature's most adept survival machines. I've long maintained that the stand hunter lives on Whitetail Time and that's a pace I've come to cherish.

STILL-HUNTING AND TRACKING TECHNIQUES

Gusty winds and a light drizzle seemed my only company on the raw November morning. It was peak rut, and I'd slipped to my treestand like a ghost in the predawn. After hanging my bow and a daypack, I settled in to wait for a sunup that never came. Even when legal shooting hours arrived, the sky brightened only to a dull, steely gray. And then the rain came.

While the overcast sky and mist weren't cheery, I actually like such conditions. Light-shy bucks often travel well on mornings when sun-loving creatures (like people) stay in bed. So I wriggled into raingear, screwed up my optimism and vowed to tough things out. Four hours later I hadn't seen a single whitetail.

Fortitude is fine, so long as it's based on realism. But as my vigil entered its fifth hour I was forced into some analytical thinking. I knew that the rut was popping and that many does were now in estrus. Perhaps the massive 12-point I was hunting had found one of them. If so, he would not be on the seeking mission I'd envisioned; he'd have his love interest pinned down in tight cover so he could breed her without competition.

There was another reality to consider, as well. The landowner had granted permission for four men to bowhunt this farm during the past week. They'd likely put my buck, and every whitetail on the property, on alert during their six-day assault. Encountering such pressure would make deer reluctant to move regardless of the conditions.

Defeated by these thoughts, or perhaps just the constant pelting of rain on my hood, I decided to crawl out of my tree. I needed relief—or at least coffee—to keep my mind in the game. But somehow the truck was not where I wanted to go. The rut is a fleeting event, and I wring it for every drop of excitement I can. Though the treestand wasn't working, I couldn't bring myself to give up. But it was time for a change of pace.

I'd seen just enough of the 12-point and his sign to know his bedding areas, and the wind was perfect for a still-hunt through one of them. Shedding my daypack, tree steps, and some extra clothing, I hiked to the spine of a long, timbered ridge. Dense stands of red cedar, prickly ash, and downed oak tops lay on the end of the ridge. This was one of the buck's favorite hangouts, and I began to sneak slowly toward it.

It takes some adjustment—in both mindset and pace—to switch from waiting for deer to walking at them. With a bow in hand, I knew that in order to shoot my buck I'd have to see him first, and that meant moving at a crawl and stopping frequently to let my eyes dissect the cover. The wet terrain allowed me to move in relative quiet and the wind slid across my cheek, but those were my only advantages.

I bumped the first deer, of course. I'd just congratulated my-self on my snail's pace and foxy stealth when I looked up to see a small deer flagging as it bounded downhill. My muffled curse was directed inward and not at the buck fawn; he was playing the game for keeps, I was out for a stroll. And, I reminded myself, that's all I'd be accomplishing if I didn't slow things down. After reaching the fawn's bed, I stopped for a while, eating a candy bar and scanning the cover ahead for the best path to the end of the ridge.

One hundred yards after my snack break I saw my second deer; a doe bedded tight to a cedar tree. She was looking away from me and so perfectly camouflaged I'd never have spotted her except that she repeatedly twitched her right ear. When the movement finally registered I trained my binoculars on her sil-houette. I was nearing the buck's bedroom, and if I bumped this deer she could bolt through his sanctuary and all would be lost. So I sat again for a time, picking out a route that would get me past the doe's eyes and ears. Twenty rain-soaked minutes later I was drawing even with her when she rose, shook off, and ambled away, nibbling acorns. "Okay," I mumbled to myself, "you got lucky there. Now for the big dog."

I knew I'd catch a break as I neared the end of the ridge. An old logging trail came up from the bottom of the hill and extended some seventy-five yards along the ridgetop. Spring scouting sessions had revealed that bucks liked to bed in the thick cover on either side of the skid trail. Once I reached the path, I reasoned, I'd have silent, effortless walking. Then it would just be a question of whether the buck was there and who spotted whom first.

For me, the difficulty of still-hunting is less about physical mechanics and more about the mental requirements to execute it for extended periods. Moving quietly and scanning for deer isn't nearly as tough as maintaining the concentration to do so. I'm primarily a treestand hunter who's spent the better part of two decades programming my mind to deal with long periods of numbness. Get me two hours into a still-hunt and I feel like I'm in the thick of a graduate-level pass/fail test. So I stop and sit. A lot. Some of this is to search for deer, the rest is pure mental exhaustion.

It was during one of those rest stops that I spotted another doe. She had backed herself into a dense copse of dogwood and blackberry brush and was bedded against an oak stump. I have no idea how I saw her. I guess I'd scanned the stump often enough that it occurred to me oak stumps don't grow noses. That's all I could see with the naked eye, a black nose with a little white ring around it. But after slowly raising the binocs, the rest of her head took shape, and just behind her I could see a gosh-awful tangle of branches that looked nothing like prickly ash. And then I realized the branches were antlers attached to a very large deer that was looking right at me.

Had I been toting my old Remington slug gun, killing the buck would have been as simple as rising to one knee and delivering the payload. The deer were less than thirty steps away and had either just seen me or were counting on watching me walk right on by. I had a perfect little hole leading to the buck's shoulder that I could have easily slipped a slug through, but I worried about arrow flight in the thick cover. So I held the bow in front of my face and slid one foot closer.

That was all it took. The doe rose first, keeping her head low to avoid the dense brush. She looked like a rabbit wiggling through the prickly ash, miraculously heading toward the opening of the logging road. The cover was tight enough that she couldn't run, so her escape was a series of little hops, which the buck emulated as he rose to follow. He had even more difficulty, as his antlers hung up on brush and jerked his head back with each step. As the doe's front legs touched the logging road I drew my bow and pointed it at the middle of the trail. A second later the buck's nose filled that space and I aimed in front of his leg and released. The arrow nicked hair off the top of the buck's shoulder, then buried itself in a cherry sapling beyond him. The pair scuffed and slid down the dirt trail as they made good their escape.

I have wanted few deer in my life as much as that buck. Not so much for his antler size (which was tremendous; a neighbor later killed him in the gun season and taped him at 170-plus), but for the relationship I'd had with him. I'd hunted the buck all fall and seen him three times before my miss. Watching my trophy tear down that hill, something told me I'd encountered him for the last time that season.

Still, it was a wonderful way to end the relationship. I'd made a bold, aggressive move in my campaign; jumping out of my tree to actively seek out the deer I'd previously hoped to kill only by waiting for him to make a mistake. To have come so close under such circumstances gave me more delight than disappointment.

117

In the many years since, I've continued to still-hunt when conditions are right. This age-old tactic is a viable, exciting option when it's clear that whitetails—especially pressured deer—are not coming to you.

TAKING THE HUNT TO THE DEER

Perhaps no one knows this better than my friend R. G. "Dick" Bernier. Dick is an avid and highly successful deer hunter from Maine. Stand hunters like me drive Dick crazy as we hang from tree trunks like arthritic squirrels, waiting for deer to pass by. Dick is not one to sit and wait for things to happen in the whitetail woods. He kills his bucks by using the timeless and simple—yet highly difficult—techniques of still-hunting and tracking. There may be no more challenging methods for the hunter who wants to consistently kill mature whitetails. Yet Dick embraces that challenge and continues to score.

Much has been written about tracking whitetails in articles about the legendary Benoit family, and in articles and books penned by Dick Bernier himself. I've been reading such stories and admiring these techniques for many years. But for a long time I held two perceptions about them that I believe are shared by many deer hunters: (1) hunting in this manner can only be done in the vast wilds of the Northeast and (2) it requires snow.

Obviously, such a perception marginalized the methods. What if you lived outside this region and never saw white stuff? What possible application could the skills of a Dick Bernier have for a hunter living in Kansas? Or Alabama? Or Michigan?

After many hours chatting with Dick, I now believe the applications are broad. Still-hunting is viewed as an antiquated, nearly forgotten tactic only because hunters have allowed that to

Dick Bernier has perfected the art of tracking. (Dick Bernier photo)

happen. I'm doing my best to save up my attempts at social commentary until I'm a certificd Old Fart, but I'm seasoned enough to know this: As a nation, we're growing physically soft. We drive when we could walk, use power tools instead of sweat, and seek comfort instead of challenge. I don't believe there is anything wrong with these wonderful benefits of civilized life. Except that sometimes we rob ourselves of opportunity for the sake of ease.

An easy example is treestand hunting, which in recent years is the most frequently used method for tagging a whitetail. The tactic is so widespread that if you talk to a man these days who kills his deer from the ground—even if it's from a blind—it's hard not to go slack-jawed at his ingenuity and zeal. But the truth is, it was only a few decades ago that most of the nation's deer kill

Despite the fact that stand hunters account for most of the whitetails taken in North America, stalking can still put deer on the meat pole. (Dick Bernier photo)

came from ground-pounders. They tracked deer. They still-hunted deer. They stalked them. "Stands" were rocks, stumps, and blowdowns that were manned for a few hours, then abandoned when a hunter tired of waiting and decided to "walk up" his buck. Such methods aren't ancient history, they were the norm only a generation ago.

Naturally, there's no question that treestands are effective. But they are also a more or less lazy way to hunt. You put up your stand, you walk a familiar path to and from it each day, and you repeat the process until your tag is filled. It is deer hunting, but it is just one form of it—and not always the most effective one.

If you've read this far, you'll know I've killed the vast majority of my bucks from an elevated platform, so I'm pitching rocks at my own glass house when I say that more of us need to climb down from the trees and challenge ourselves to learn more about hunting. Still-hunting—moving slowly and quietly through cover, attempting to slip up on deer for a shot—is one of those methods.

Tracking, it can be argued, is the highest form of the sport. To cut a whitetail track in the snow, then follow that path to the deer and kill him, is challenge exemplified.

It is also the quintessential hunt for pressured deer, as it's common for a tracker to pursue a buck that, at some point at least, becomes aware of the hunter on his tail. Consequently, the buck is not going about his business, he is trying to save his skin. Given the intelligence and survival skills possessed by mature bucks, I can think of no harder-won trophy than a whitetail taken by this method.

There are many areas where tracking is not a viable practice; places where hunter densities make the technique unsafe or where myriad property lines render it illegal. But thankfully this technique can be applied in many more states than the northern New England region where it is most widely practiced.

Anyplace with relatively large tracts of land and reduced hunting pressure offers the best opportunities for a deer tracker. But as Dick Bernier has pointed out to me on several occasions, even if a hunter can't track in his area, there is still much he can learn from a tracker. Stand hunters, still-hunters, and even folks who drive deer can benefit from the ancient art of reading deer sign—and this includes every hunter who chases pressured whitetails.

To that end, let's take a look at some of the knowledge and techniques that Dick has perfected in over thirty years of hard, passionate hunting.

121

THE STILL-HUNTER:
STEALTH PERSONIFIED

Dick employs still-hunting whenever snow prevents him from using his favorite tactic of tracking, which, given the odd weather in recent years, has been quite often. But rather than view still-hunting and tracking as separate skills, Dick sees them as inexorably linked.

"I believe you can't be a good tracker without first having the skills of the still-hunter," Dick stresses. "Writer T. S. Van Dyke described still-hunting as 'a combination of skills,' which included moving slowly across the landscape, searching for deer, reading tracks and other sign, and stalking deer when they were spotted. All those skills come into play for both the still-hunter and the tracker."

According to Dick, the reason most hunters fail at still-hunting is that they simply move too quickly. "Still-hunting boils down to this: a man enters the woods looking for a buck, and who sees whom first often determines the outcome. If you're moving too quickly, you not only rob your eyes of the chance to scan cover and search for deer, you give whitetails the opportunity to spot you first. Over the years I've come to believe that deer are farsighted, which explains why they frequently stop and stare at us when we believe they should be running. I'm convinced that they just don't see as well as we think they do. My proof has come while hunting in swirling snow. You can creep dangerously close to deer in those conditions simply because their vision is blurred by the flakes; they look right at you and cannot see you as long as you move slowly. Deer are spooked not so much by movement, but by movement that to them is unnatural."

The key to still-hunting is infinite patience. Move very slowly and stop often to scan cover. (Pat Reeve photo)

Another reason that hopeful still-hunters fail is because they don't look for deer on their level, Dick says. "Looking for bedded deer is a classic example. When bedded, the top of a deer will only be eighteen to twenty inches off the ground. Most of the time, the only way you're going to spot that deer is if you're on your knees. And let me tell you, it's hard work to get down there a hundred times in the course of a full day of hunting. Especially when you're my age."

Paying attention to the wind is another hurdle for the still-hunter. "The vision of a whitetail can be beat," Dick says. "And you can be quiet enough to fool his ears. But you can never beat his nose. I'd never disparage another hunter's methods or his gear, but I shake my head at some of the money that is spent on scent-control products. I know they help reduce odor. But is it enough to completely beat a whitetail's nose? I'm skeptical. In my book, to be a successful whitetail hunter you have to pay attention to the wind or you're finished. When I'm still-hunting, I strive to keep that wind either on my cheek or moving across it all the time. If I can pull that off, I can walk right up on a deer. If I can't . . . well, it doesn't matter what else I do."

So much for how *not* to still-hunt. To pull off this method, Dick focuses on areas he knows hold mature deer. In the heavily timbered areas of the Northeast, that frequently translates into areas of timber cutting, where high-quality browse and other feed are associated with logging. Then he enters the woods—into the wind, of course—and moves through likely cover.

In his book *On the Track*, Dick describes the hunt like this: "I don't need snow to tell me I've got deer out there. There's other signs indicating that . . . [and it's the] same on snow as it is

Still-hunters must learn to spot perfectly camouflaged deer—even if it's only a yearling or fawn—before they are themselves spotted.

on leaves. [A buck] will roll the leaves over where other deer won't. His droppings will tend to be larger, and if he's done any rubbing or scraping, all the better. It doesn't take me long to prove whether a large buck is about.

"I've seen hunters parade right past some wonderful indicators and then claim they haven't seen anything to warrant their return . . . You have to be observant. Look for the least little disturbances, they're all clues . . . When I enter the woods to stalk a buck, I prefer to act just exactly like him . . . if he's not spooked or jumped, he has no set pattern. I may go right, then left, depending on the wind. If someone were trailing me, walking in my footsteps, they might have a hard time figuring out what I'm doing. I always try to mix up my travel route, and if I revisit that same area on another day, the course I take is usually in a different direction.

"My every step is taken with the thought that my bare feet are being placed on crushed glass. Occasionally I'll make a noise, but not continuously or often . . . What I'm looking at for deer sign will determine how far and how fast my travel becomes. If the area is littered with fresh droppings, tracks, and especially buck activity, I'll slow to a crawl, tearing apart the landscape with my eyes. If I don't see anything to my satisfaction, I'll take off and go until what I'm after is located. . . . Some days, less than a handful of miles will be covered with a buck right under my nose, and on others I can go on and on and accomplish nothing. It all depends on what the buck is up to. These are the things you have to consider when you enter the woods. We've done our homework and know where the big bucks reside, but that's no guarantee we're going to come out with one. He may take off for another area . . . and his wanderings will be found to give me lots of exercise that day."

Dick has killed numerous bucks by employing his keen skill and endless patience, but he describes one of his most memorable days in his wonderful book *The Deer Trackers*. "I was on bare ground with only freshly soaked leaves for tracking. I had made my way to the top of a good-sized ridge and I was silently easing down the opposite side, zigzagging. I found where a buck had walked through not long before. His hooves were really cutting down through those leaves, and therefore he was worth following. The hard part of tracking on bare ground is that you are forced to look at the ground far more often than on snow.

These tracks are easy to see, but you must judge their age and the size of the deer that made them before deciding if they're worth following. (Dick Bernier photo)

"As I followed him down below the mid part of the ridge he stayed in the hardwood. I lost his track three different times and had to circle until I picked it up again. He was just meandering, with no real purpose. After picking up his trail for the third time, I proceeded a short distance when I spotted one quick flash of white between a crotch in a big beech tree. My first thought was that it was a snowy owl, since we had seen a couple of them in the past few weeks. I really had not expected to be this close to the buck yet.

"Nevertheless, my rifle was up as that flicker of white suddenly turned into an antler, then a set of antlers and a nose. I did not want to shoot him in the head so I waited. All he had to do was step to the left or right. If he went straight he would be down the ridge with the beech tree blocking my view. The ball was in his court. 'Your move,' I muttered to myself as I watched a trace of vapors emitted from his nostrils. At this point I needed to stay calm. He did not know I was near. Finally, after what seemed an eternity, the buck stepped to his left and filled my peep sight. He dressed out at 218 pounds and carried 8 points."

TRACKING DEER: WHERE SKILL, KNOWLEDGE, AND PERSISTENCE MEET

For most hunters, the prospect of tracking a whitetail buck and killing him seems an impossible task. The doubt of these hunters is understandable, for by the time a buck has reached maturity, he has molded his existence into a very small and tightly regulated hierarchy that is ranked something like this: (1)

stay alive; (2) eat and drink; (3) breed does. There are rare moments when a buck rearranges this order to place breeding above all else, but such chaos is not to be counted on. Confront even the randiest buck with danger and he will recall his priorities in a hurry, at least long enough to live another day.

So how does a Dick Bernier enter the world of such a survival machine—an animal who is not only on his home turf, but whose nose, ears, and legs are infinitely superior to his pursuer—and come out with a trophy? "By out-thinking him," Dick stresses. "The only tool we have that can beat a buck is our brain. Unfortunately, we engage it so infrequently."

My friend is talking tongue in cheek, but only a little. Listen to Dick tell deer stories long enough and you will hear of bucks that bested him for miles or days, only to wind up on the camp meat pole. It would have been easy to give up on such crafty prey, but in each case the hunter remained persistent, observed patterns the buck displayed, and capitalized on them. Dick is a fine shot, an excellent woodsman, and keeps himself in top shape, but even he admits these attributes are not enough to top a wise old buck. But Dick's years of experience and dogged determination make for a deadly combination.

Like still-hunting, tracking was once a common technique among whitetail hunters. But as large habitats became fragmented and unsuitable for tracking—and sportsmen found less rigorous and time-consuming methods to pursue deer—the vital skills needed for the method were being gradually lost. Among these skills is the ability to distinguish tracks and read sign. As an ambassador for both the sport and his techniques, Dick is more than happy to share the fundamentals of his craft.

"The first step is learning to tell a buck's track from a doe's," Dick says. "To start, a buck track—even that of a one-and-a-half year-old—will always toe-out, and a doe track never will. Her track will be straight on or slightly toed-in. But the most distinguishing characteristic is urine markings in the snow. Does will squat and pee between or slightly behind their back legs into a relatively small area. A buck will always leave a series of dribbles in the track as he finishes and begins to walk. All males—human, dog, whatever—will do the same thing. You see a deer track with dribbles between the tracks and it's a buck, guaranteed."

Next, of course, is deciphering a mature buck—the object of Dick's pursuit—from a younger animal. Knowing that he may be on a track for several hours before seeing its maker, Dick wants to be sure he's following a mature animal. "Width is one of the most important indicators," he notes. "My fist is 3¼ inches across the back, and if I can fit my fist into a track, I know I'm onto a good deer. Track depth is another indicator. If the buck makes a deep impression compared to other deer, he's a heavy animal. I've found track length to be one of the poorest indicators; some big deer simply have short feet, or their [hooves] could be broomed off on rocky soil."

Dick feels the ability to read such spoor is invaluable to all deer hunters, even those who cannot still-hunt or track in their area. "Any place where a hunter has snow on the ground for at least a portion of the season, he can use tracking skills to put himself in position to kill a trophy buck," he says. "If you have only a hundred acres that's bordered by private land, you can follow a buck's track as he moves through your property. Observe how he uses the terrain, where he feeds, beds, rubs, and scrapes. Then set your stand accordingly."

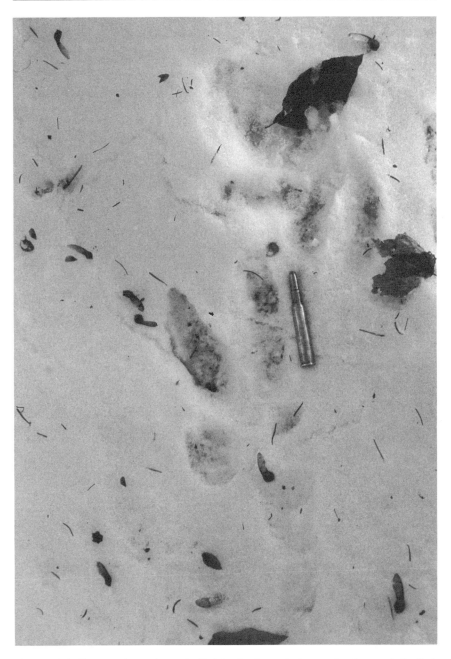

This track indicates a large, heavy-bodied buck—just what every tracker wants to find. Note that the toes point slightly outward. (Dick Bernier photo)

Once a buck track is discovered, Dick determines its freshness, often by comparing it to his own track and the snow conditions. If he feels he can catch up to the deer within a few hours he takes up the trail. Again, as in still-hunting, Dick lets the deer determine the pace. "If he's making a beeline somewhere, I keep after him. But once that track starts to wander, I'm on full alert. He may have only paused to browse or rub or make a scrape, then went off on another jaunt. But you don't know that; he could be right up ahead. When I see a track start to slow, I do the same; I'm still-hunting, I'm living completely in the moment, wondering if I can see him in the cover ahead."

Naturally, even the most experienced trackers overrun their quarry and bump a buck now and then. That's when even the most skilled hunter is put to the test. "Their first response when you spook them is to flee," Dick notes. "What happens after that is, I'm convinced, largely a part of the deer's personality. Some will put miles on in a straight line; I prefer to just let those deer go, as I'll never catch up with them. But generally, a whitetail is like a large rabbit, most of the escape moves he makes are in a circular pattern. The circles are larger, of course. But the pattern is the same."

Dick has seen whitetails run directly to water, such as a stream or river, and walk in it for a half-mile before slipping out on a bank. "Water represents safety to deer," he says. "They don't know we can't smell, all they do know is that they have a predator on their tail and they're trying to lose their scent trail. I've had bucks stop, walk backward directly in their own track, and then leap far to the side of the trail. I remember thinking 'I'm tracking a reindeer here.' Some will make a wide circle, come back to a

Cagey bucks will use a variety of tricks to elude pursuit. Read sign carefully to get a handle on how they are reacting to the pressure. (Dick Bernier photo)

high knob or ridge, and just stand there watching their backtrail. And sometimes an animal that is bothered, pestered, and harangued enough will even get curious and come looking for this thing that won't leave him alone."

Summarizing all the behaviors that a whitetail buck with a tracker on his tail will resort to would require not only a hefty book, but an ongoing series. "The important thing to remember is to keep your mind engaged all the time," Dick stresses. "You have to be aware of patterns the deer is showing you. Remember, a buck cannot think things through. He is only going to repeat behaviors that have worked for him. If you can notice those behaviors, sometimes you can capitalize on them and kill the deer. But even if you don't tag the buck, you will have learned something, and perhaps you can use it in the future, either on this buck or another one. I've been doing this for many years and I'm still learning. That's part of the art; the more you learn, the more proficient you become."

Dick has recounted many memorable whitetail hunts in his books *The Deer Trackers* and *On the Track* (available by calling Dick at 207-892-3682), and I recommend these wonderful books to any serious deer hunter. Among my favorite tales was of a buck Dick tracked for over six hours one wintry November day. After removing his boots and socks to follow the buck and his companion doe across a frigid river, Dick dried his feet, slipped his socks and boots back on, and dogged their trail as the whitetails crossed clearcuts and wandered among snow-covered conifers. Emerging from such a wintry jungle, Dick shook the white stuff off his shoulders and realized he was running out of daylight—and suitable conditions—to catch his prize.

"The snow was falling harder now and the urgency of remaining close . . . became much more important. His tracks were starting to get snowed in. The doe led him and now me into a barnyard of tracks that circled, re-circled, and literally went in every direction. For a while I was able to stay with my buck, but as the tracks continued to fill in it became almost impossible. I would follow a set that I thought were his and soon realize they were not . . . Having gone in so many circles I actually felt like a beagle dog on a rabbit run. Frustrated, I stood motionless in the falling snow, trying to determine my next move.

"Finally, I decided to make a large circle in hope of locating that distinguishable track . . . his very recognizable splayed imprints, snowed in as they were, proved it was him. Much to my

After a long stalk, it feels good to know that it was your skill that put you in position to take a solid buck like this one. (Pat Reeve photo)

surprise and chagrin, his track led [into a cedar grove] in a direction that placed the wind at his back. Entering into this almost impenetrable, uninviting terrain required me to become a contortionist. Bending, twisting, and even crawling at times became the necessary moves. His track, as well as an assortment of other doe tracks, were found within this sanctuary and all appeared smoking fresh. It was difficult to believe that an animal of this size was able to weave his way through this tangle . . .

"Forced onto hands and knees, I stuck my left leg through the opening he had passed through. Dragging my upper body in one fluid motion, I spotted his fresh, and recently vacated, bed. My eyes followed the tracks leading away . . . five, ten, fifteen, twenty yards was mentally calculated when suddenly, for the first time, he appeared . . . and was walking stiff-leggedly back on his tracks. His head and horns swung defiantly from side to side . . . Apparently, he figured another buck had invaded his domain, and judging from his actions, he didn't appear happy about it. From that same position, not daring to move, I eased the carbine pump to my shoulder. At a distance of twelve steps . . . the stillness was broken with the roar of my '06. In what seemed like slow motion . . . my buck just sort of melted to the ground."

GEAR AND SAFETY CONSIDERATIONS FOR THE STILL-HUNTER

Obviously, the gear and clothing choices of a mobile hunter will be far different than those of stand hunter. "You gotta go light," Dick stresses. "You will be moving for the better part of a day, and any extra weight you carry will not only slow you down, it will make you less effective as you battle its bulk. I begin with a light pair of polypropylene long underwear next to my body. Over that I slip a chamois shirt, followed by a deer-tracker jacket made of wool and a pair of wool pants. I love wool clothing because it's soft, warm, and silent. And it can take a beating like no other fabric." In areas where it's required, and/or in zones where hunter densities demand it, Dick will don a blaze orange vest over his wool.

Boots are another special consideration. "Light boots are essential for me, as I like to feel what's under my feet. I spent years trying different boots until I settled on what I think is the ideal model for the still-hunter/tracker. It's made by the Muck Company, and it's called the Woody Max. It has a rubber bottom and neoprene upper. When they were first recommended to me you couldn't have found a bigger skeptic. But they are comfortable, lightweight, and durable beyond belief. I've never found their equal."

Dick's preferred firearm is a Remington 760, a pump-action carbine that is light to carry and easy to shoulder. "It weighs 6½ pounds fully loaded and equipped with a sling," he notes. "But I use the sling only to carry my rifle at the end of the day; the rest of the time it's in my hands, ready for action."

The dense cover Dick hunts makes optics impractical, so he mounts a Williams peep sight equipped with a screw-in reticle. "That's what I've been shooting for thirty-four seasons and it's what I'm comfortable with," he says. "I can find a deer quickly in it and it's fail-safe."

Beyond clothing and his weapon, Dick carries little else. "I have a ball-style compass pinned to my coat, and a backup I carry on a lanyard around my neck," he says. "I carry a knife, a length of rope for dragging, matches, and fire-starting material. I have never had to spend a night out in the woods, but I'm prepared to if that situation arises."

Dick acknowledges that many hunters fear getting lost in the big-woods environments he hunts. "We deal with that by driving every logging road in our hunting area to familiarize ourselves with them," he says. "That way, when I enter a block of timber I know where the roads are. I constantly refer to my compass as I hunt and [visualize] where I am in that section of woods. When it's time to quit for the day, I follow my compass to the nearest road. I would much rather walk several extra miles to reach my truck on a road than stumble through the woods in the dark. Besides, I am usually hunting with my father, son, or friend, and if one of us doesn't show up at the truck at dark, we get in the truck and go looking for him, based on our knowledge of where he's hunting that day."

For hunters accustomed to more civilized environments, or the sedentary comforts of a stand or blind, Dick's aggressive, highly mobile tactics may seem too intimidating or challenging. Yet this veteran woodsman not only perseveres, he wishes others would join him. "The areas we hunt are open to the public," he says. "Anyone can hunt them for the same price I can and learn the same skills I did. Many people have told me I have a special gift or skill, but I truly don't. I've said for years that if I can do this, anyone can. All you need is the love of a challenge and a desire to learn. I strongly believe that all hunters have a built-in yearning for adventure and excitement, for conquering and enduring. Those qualities are built into how I hunt. The man with lots of money in his pocket will topple far more big bucks than I ever will. But he won't do it in the same manner. And I don't know how he could love it any more than I do. How I hunt is part of who I am."

6

BOWHUNTING TACTICS

I have hunted long enough to believe that some animals give themselves to a hunter, yielding to our harvest as an almost inevitable event. This is something I can't explain without sounding mystical. All I know is what I've seen. On some hunts, I can do absolutely everything right and the deer elude me. On others, well—I'll use the first buck I ever killed with a bow as an example.

I was a high school senior with a Friday off in early November. My buddy Tim and I wanted nothing more than to spend that precious vacation day in the deer woods. So we drove in the predawn to a public hunting area only thirty miles from our homes. With the rut in high gear, we planned to hunt all day, praying that one of the bucks we'd seen that fall would make a mistake. We were not trophy hunters then; killing any buck with a bow would not only have satisfied us, it would have sent us into orbit.

Tim and I had several treestand setups located on a vast riverbottom area, but that morning we decided to wing it. We slipped into a small oxbow of timber that we'd scouted but never hunted before. Dawn was breaking as we left Tim's battered, lime-green Mercury Bobcat at the parking lot and snuck into the tangle of alder, willow, and river birch a quarter mile away. Tim knew where he wanted to hunt, and after a short walk he departed along a well-used deer trail. I proceeded down another path, looking for a likely place to hang my stand. I wasn't exactly bumbling, but I was certainly not being stealthy.

I practically bumped into the blowdown. It was an old river birch that had tipped over in a windstorm, lying conveniently within bow range of two deer trails. With sunrise only minutes away, I knew I didn't have time to look for a better spot. Just before wriggling into the blowdown, I saturated a small rag with some deer scent and hung it on a nearby branch about chest high. Then I clambered into the fallen tree, snapping limbs to clear a sitting area. The breaking twigs shattered the morning silence, and I cussed myself for the racket. "You aren't going to kill anything," I mumbled. "But the least you could do is not screw things up for your partner."

Looking back on my impromptu brush-clearing with the benefit of a couple decades of experience, I now realize my ruckus actually attracted the whitetail. Rutting bucks frequently find other deer by sound alone and will often run to investigate any "deer" they hear in their domain. But on that morning, all I knew was that one moment I was scolding myself, and the next I was looking at an 8-point buck walking toward my setup like I'd pulled on his tether.

To seal the deal, the buck smelled my scent rag at about forty paces. I had, fortunately, collected my wits enough to nock an arrow and point it toward the approaching deer. Within seconds he was standing broadside at nine steps, his nose snuffling my rag like the Secret of Life was soaked in its folds.

The buck never flinched as I drew, settled my sight pin on his body, and released. I had never encountered a buck at eye level at such close range before, and I remember thinking "there's no way I can miss." Of course, the worst moments a teenager experiences are those when he realizes he actually knows only a fraction of the stuff he thinks he does, and that thought was a certified Worst Moment. Over the years I've proved time and again that there are plenty of ways to miss easy shots, but I'm more humble now. I thought my world had ended when I missed that poke-n-hope.

But the deer didn't seem to mind much. He did hop off a couple of yards, then turn—still broadside—and lift his head to stare curiously at my blowdown. I was paralyzed for several seconds, but eventually decided I had absolutely nothing to lose by nocking another arrow. "What else can you do but spook him again?" my jeering inner voice asked.

So I slid my hand toward my bow quiver and plucked out an arrow, staring at the buck's eyes for a reaction. Nothing. Then I snuck the shaft alongside the bow's riser and snapped the nock onto the string. An eye blink. Easing the bow up like it was made of crystal, I drew and anchored, fully expecting that this motion would turn the buck inside out. Nada. This time I centered the little green pin on the buck's ribcage and released.

The buck blew out, my red-and-yellow fletching sticking from his ribs as he ran. Two hours later, Tim and I were dragging the handsome buck out to the car; a couple of high school boys who couldn't have been prouder if they'd scored the winning touchdown at the homecoming football game.

THE IRONY OF BOWHUNTING PRESSURED DEER

The memory of that hunt remains one of my most precious. Not only did it mark my first archery buck, but one that came from an extremely difficult place to hunt. That place was a state-owned wildlife area just north of Davenport, Iowa, and it was the stereotypical public hunting ground of the 1970s. Parking lots were often strewn with litter and shotshells, road signs pulled double-duty as targets for slugs and small arms fire, and on the weekends a steady stream of hunters stormed in to chase ducks and geese, pheasant and quail, rabbits and squirrels.

Tim and I were there for the whitetails. We were anomalies in our high school; clean-cut boys who didn't get drunk or act defiant, but who lived to hunt and fish and trap. Our obsessions seemed odd to most of our classmates, big-city boys who wouldn't know a broadhead from a bowling ball and who thought a stand was the thing that held up a Christmas tree. But Tim and I were undaunted. We shot our bows, read about deer, and actually prayed for the start of school every year—which meant the archery season was soon to open.

We had tried for the better part of two years to secure permission on private property. Driving country roads in the summer, we'd find a farm with a woodlot or a timbered creek bottom and make the long, slow drive up the lane. The farmers were, to a man, friendly and understanding. But you could see the doubt in their eyes. We came from the big city, the same city that every slob hunter—the ones who'd shot a sign or left a gate open or driven across a hayfield—had come from. The answer we received each time was a firm but polite "No."

So we settled on the wildlife area, a huge acreage that butted hard against the Mississippi River and was loved by duck hunters. Water was everywhere on this tract—small ponds and old irrigation ditches and even a couple of creeks and a river that flowed among lowland timber and cattails. The conservation department had planted food plots wherever it was dry enough, which usually meant close to the road. At first we scouted the area with the firm conviction that our main goal should be to get away from the parking lots. We were young and strong and had never let physical effort hamper our desire to get anywhere. So we loaded our gear on our backs and headed as deep into the swamp as we dared.

It was a good strategy, except that it often took us right to the duck hunters. Twice I had the shot from nearby duck blinds rain down on me while I sat in my treestand. We'd placed those stands without knowing that the waterfowl guys could leave a boat landing and in minutes motor to the same spot we'd hiked a mile to. So we gave up on hard walking and decided to hunt smart instead; looking for small pockets of cover isolated from boat traffic and cars and the hunters who were never far away from their transportation.

That's why that first buck was so sweet. It had come after so much difficulty and frustration and plain hard work. We didn't know this at the time, either, but hunting that wildlife area was excellent training for our future. Not only did we learn to adjust to the movement and behavior of other hunters, we were forced to learn how whitetails did the very same thing.

Bowhunting pressured whitetails isn't a topic that gets a lot of attention these days. Perhaps it's because the archery season is typically thought of as an idyllic, early-fall pursuit that precedes the frenetic gun opener. Whitetails are either in their early-season feeding patterns or in the frenzy of the rut. And, of course, the number of bowhunters in the woods usually represents a fraction of the sportsmen who participate in the gun season.

Bow season is seen as a lazy, contemplative time when all a hunter has to do is figure out local deer patterns, hang a treestand, and wait for an opportunity. But in many areas, the deer that archers pursue are under moderate to intense pressure throughout the fall. Public areas like the one I started in are but one example. There are special- or limited-entry hunts where bowhunters must not only score in a tight timeframe, but compete with other archers to do so. There are suburban hunting opportunities where deer may quietly watch a woman working in her garden but sprint from a camouflaged figure hiking to a treestand. And no matter where a bowhunter chases deer, there is collateral pressure in the form of small game and waterfowl hunters, hikers, horseback (and mountain bike and ATV) riders, and even birders. All share our love for the autumn woods—and have the right to do so—yet they ensure that the deer we hunt will be on high alert and ever mindful of their safety.

Bowhunters face stiffer competition these days—forcing them to deal with pressured deer that sometimes react like the firearms season has already started.

The challenge for a bowhunter in such a situation is considerable. But it's possible to succeed, provided certain techniques and practices are understood and carried out.

Let's take a look at some hunters who've been successful hunting pressured whitetails during the bow season and see how they scored.

STAN POTTS: ILLINOIS PUBLIC LAND LEGEND

Hunters who believe the terms "public area" and "trophy whitetail" are mutually exclusive terms have not heard about Stan Potts. This friendly, energetic Illinois archer has tagged dozens of mature whitetails, and some of his best have come

Stan Potts uses thorough scouting, a solid game plan, and mental toughness to take trophy whitetails on public land. (Pat Reeve photo)

from public hunting areas. While it's true these bucks were taken in the Land of Lincoln—a state well known for producing monster deer—it is also true that the bucks he's killed on public land have lived in areas where the pressure is constant from the season opener to closing day. Stan's knowledge of whitetail behavior and his ability to develop a sound game plan have allowed him to emerge from some hard-hunted areas with a trophy.

"I guess the biggest hurdle to clear when hunting public land is the mental one," Stan stresses. "People think, 'It's public access, so there's no big bucks,' and that's simply not true. Granted, I go out of my way to look for areas where there are some restrictions—like an archery-only area—but that's because I want to harvest a mature deer. That just assures me that there will be mature bucks in the herd. I need to have that confidence to hunt hard, because even in the best areas, truly mature bucks will represent just a fraction of the population."

Stan feels strongly that he's succeeded because he scouts his areas thoroughly, constructs a game plan for hunting them, and does his best to ignore the presence of other hunters. "Let's face it, Midwestern deer contend with people from the day they're born," he says. "There are farmers, hikers, hunters, whatever. If whitetails spooked every time they saw, heard, or smelled someone, they'd never stop running. So deer, especially big bucks, quickly learn to tell the difference between people who represent a threat, and people who don't. I do my best to hunt the most careful way I know how and ignore what other people are doing. I can only control what I do, I can't control other hunters. So I just block 'em out of my head."

To illustrate, Stan points to a memorable buck he plucked from an Illinois public tract. "I was set up in a prime stand spot during the peak of the rut," he recalls. "I knew this place was good and the sign was everywhere. I was only a couple of hours into a morning hunt when I heard something coming over the ridge. It was a pair of hunters who were already quitting for the day. They even lingered in my area, only thirty yards away, pointing to all the great buck sign. And then they left. Now I know how a lot of hunters would have reacted right then; they'd have been disgusted, figured things were ruined for the day, and headed out. But I stuck with it, and within a half hour I heard something else coming through the leaves, from the same direction those hunters had gone. It was a massive 5x5, and he wasn't on the run, he was looking for does. I made the shot. He scored 164, Pope & Young."

Stan develops his game plan by studying aerial photos of an area in the preseason. "I start by marking the perimeter of the hunting area with a pencil," he says. "And then I start looking for funnels and pinch points that I know big bucks are going to travel once the rut starts. I like an area where three or four ridges come together, the end of a fenceline in the timber, a big bend in a creek, the back corner of a field, or any place where two types of habitat meet. Those are the kinds of places that big bucks cruise through, looking for does.

"Once I locate eight or ten spots like that, I circle them on the map and then I go walk them. The best time to do that is in the off-season, which is right after hunting ends until green-up. I'm looking for two things; big buck sign and, if I find that, the perfect tree to put a stand in. If I visit all ten of these spots, maybe only five or six will have the sign I need, which is big rubs and scrapes. If the sign isn't there, I don't go back. But if it is, I look for a stand tree that will put me twenty yards or less from where I think that buck will travel through the funnel. I consider prevailing winds, which in Illinois are usually southwest if the weather pattern is steady and northwest if a front's pushing through. I want to have a couple options for different wind directions."

Once his stand sites are located, Stan stays out of the hunting areas until October 25, which represents the general start of the "seeking" phase of the rut. "You can go in earlier and kill a buck," Stan says. "People do it every year. But I believe that your chances of alerting a resident buck—one that's living in your stand area—are high. And unless you kill him right away, he's going to learn you're there and avoid the area. These big ones remember; even if a hot doe trots right past your stand and that big one is on her tail, he'll detour around that spot. So I'm just in-

Knowing when to use a particular stand is as important as scouting out the site itself.

creasing my odds if I stay out of there. I don't want to hunt just bucks that have come in from far away. I want them *plus* the resident deer."

Stan does rely on some summer reconnaissance missions to glass his areas for bachelor groups of bucks. "I stay well off the fields and bring a spotting scope," he says. "And I watch the general areas where my stands are. If I see four or five shooter bucks coming out to feed in July and August, just think what that does for my confidence come fall. Sure, some of those bucks are going to disperse and not be available. But some of them will be. That's all part of getting mentally ready for the season. It's just easier to hunt hard when you know what's out there, and hunting big bucks is a mental game. You're not always sitting the field edge where you'll spot a dozen deer in an evening, so you have to know the deer you're after is there."

With the arrival of late October, Stan launches his assault. "I only hunt a spot if the wind is perfect," he stresses. "And if it's right when I go in and switches on me, I get out of there. You have to do that. I put too much time in finding these spots to burn them just hoping I'll get lucky. I need to have confidence that I'm in the right stand and that the deer will move through and not bust me. I can't have that if the wind is wrong."

Stan also tries to keep a low profile when entering and exiting stands. "Sneak along the shadows instead of skylighting yourself in the field," he says. "Walk out a small depression or ditch, or along a creekbed. I'll also vary my route a little each time, maybe walking fifty or sixty yards off my last path. But you can take things too far to conceal your entry, especially in the morning. I believe you need to get to your stand in the predawn quickly and efficiently. Sneaking and slithering can alert more

deer than simply moving through purposefully. If a buck sees
you slipping and sneaking he'll go on alert and maybe bust out
of there. But walk on through, and he'll usually just stand there
and watch."

Since he's hunting top buck areas during prime time, Stan
keeps at it most of the day. "I rarely sit in one stand for an entire
day anymore," he admits. "I need to get down for an hour at midday, head back to the truck, and have a sandwich. But then I'm
right back in the saddle, often at a different stand. I've killed the
majority of my bucks between 9:30 and 2:00. I'm convinced that
big deer are just more comfortable moving then. They know
when most hunters are not in the woods."

One of Stan's most memorable trophies serves as a perfect il-
lustration of how his hunting skill and aggressive approach has
led to success on hard-hunted public lands. "I was on a public
area and had come out for a break after the morning hunt," he recalls. "I moved to another stand at about 1:00 and I'd no more
than settled in when I saw a pair of deer bedded in a picked cornfield. They were about four hundred yards from me, and when I
got the binoculars on them I could see it was a doe and a huge
buck."

Stan watched the pair for a while, then decided to take action. "We'd had rain for two days, the fields were soaked and the
wind was thirty miles per hour," he says. "So I climbed down and
started slipping toward them. They were bedded in some grass
and facing away from me, so I was able to crouch-crawl the first
two hundred yards. Then I just belly-crawled across the cornrows,
slogging through mud and water, to cut the distance. I was absolutely soaked to the bone, but I was able to work to within
twenty-five yards. When I peered over the cornstalks, I could see

a softball-size hole leading right to the buck's vitals. I kept thinking I should wait them out, but I felt I could make that shot."

Drawing the bow while holding it nearly parallel to the ground, Stan rose slowly and put his top sight pin on the buck. "I put that arrow right through that hole in the weeds and into his vitals," he says. "As they blew out of there, I could see my fletching right where I thought it should be. Within thirty yards I could tell the buck was in trouble."

When Stan recovered the buck a short time later, another hunter came running up to congratulate him. "He'd watched the whole stalk through binoculars from his treestand," Stan chuckles. "He said he'd watched the buck bed in the same field the day before and was just hoping today it would be back. He congratulated me over and over."

There was reason for celebration. Stan's giant deer was 6½ years old, field dressed at 247 pounds, and carried a 6x6 rack that scored 167.

It also serves as wonderful proof that by executing a careful game plan and remaining mentally prepared, a hunter can still tag trophy whitetails on public lands.

BILL VAZNIS:
LESSONS FROM THE GROUND

For many archers, whitetail hunting means one thing—sitting in a treestand. While the success of this technique is without question, it does—as we've examined in previous chapters—have its limitations. Far too many hunters are so married to elevated platforms that they'll walk away from prime whitetail ground if it doesn't grow suitable stand trees. I've labeled this unfortunate malady "hunting trees instead of deer."

Always scout out the best entry and exit trails for reaching your stand without alerting every deer in the area. (Bill Vaznis photo)

Bill Vaznis is a whitetail expert from New York State who is not afflicted with this curse. The veteran writer and photographer killed his first archery buck from the ground and has been a devout still-hunter ever since. Staying ground-bound has allowed Bill to arrow some wonderful deer in areas ignored by other hunters.

Bowhunters who stalk their prey have the advantage of working deer that stand hunters might never see. (Pat Reeve photo)

"I have hunted from treestands," Bill admits. "But I just don't like them very much. I'm more comfortable on the ground, and I've had success hunting that way. Ninety-eight percent of bowhunters stick with treestands, but they rule out an awful lot of good deer habitat by doing that."

Bill notes that these overlooked habitats are often places deer retreat to when under pressure from other hunters. "Whitetails quickly learn where they don't encounter people," he says. "So the areas I still-hunt are not only prime deer habitat, the bucks are in there because the hunters aren't." As an example, Bill points to an area not far from his home. "It's not far from a decent-sized town, and there are some ten thousand licensed bowhunters in that county alone. So these deer know what a bowhunter is.

"The specific area consists of a large farm on top of a hill, with alfalfa and cornfields and hardwood timber. But on the backside there is a steep hill that drops off of those fields. It's like a huge sand/gravel dune with very few trees. There are little gullies and washes, small humps and bumps, and brush-choked draws. That's where I go to still-hunt, and I always find deer."

Other areas that Bill seeks out for his still-hunts are abandoned farmsteads, creek or river bottoms, fencelines and irrigation ditches, overgrown fields, and even agricultural cropland such as cornfields. "Any place with reasonably open, but broken or uneven terrain is perfect for still-hunting," he stresses. "Other than that, I just look for the same things a stand hunter does. I want to know where the deer are bedding and feeding and get between those spots at the right time. The only difference is I'm mobile and able to move toward deer I see. To me, that's one of the

Scrapes like this one can tell you a lot about buck activity in a particular area. (Bill Vaznis photo)

biggest drawbacks to stand hunting; you can only cover a very limited area."

And, like a stand hunter, Bill relies on his ability to read and interpret buck sign to get himself in position to score. "I was hunting in Iowa a couple of years ago and found a scrape line on a public hunting area that was just smoking," he recalls. "When I looked at the scrapes, I could see that the buck was making them in the morning, as the dirt was kicked back toward the feeding area. The scrapes were along a ditch on the backside of a field and led toward a good bedding area. There were no good stand trees, so I went back to camp and told my buddy, 'I think I can kill that buck, but I have to be there at first light.'"

Dawn found Bill working slowly along the ditch, into the wind. "I was in position, just creeping along at first light," he remembers. "I heard the buck before I ever saw him, walking through the leaves along that scrape line. He was at fifty yards when I first spotted him, so I just froze and waited. That's one key to still-hunting; when you see a deer, you don't move. So the buck continued toward me, working the scrapes, and I shot him at thirty steps. He never knew what hit him. He was a 9-point that grossed in the high 140s."

Bill's trophy was particularly satisfying because there were many hunters using the public area, and it was common to see a vehicle parked every half mile along the roads surrounding the tract. But if other hunters had discovered this buck's pattern, they were avoiding the specific spot where he tagged the buck, probably due to the unique cover.

"On another hunt in Kansas, I was hunting with an outfitter who'd had me and his other hunters in treestands all season," Bill recalls. "I had my eye on this overgrown field. It was adjacent to a creek and full of briers and small pines and cedars and some old apple trees. When I asked the outfitter if he'd mind if I still-hunted that spot, he said, 'Sure.' You could see probably three hundred yards, but I had to really sneak through that old field slowly, there were so many deer.

"One evening I played hide-and-seek with a 150-class buck there. Three times I nocked an arrow, fully expecting to get the shot, but it never happened. Another evening I was able to get almost within bow range of another huge deer, but it was on a neighboring property. That buck was a solid 180-inch buck that the outfitter knew well, but his hunters just weren't seeing it. I believe those deer were in that overgrown field because they never encountered hunters."

Bill has several prime still-hunting areas, but he prefers to visit each only two or three times per week. "You can burn them out, just like you do a stand," he notes. "When you're hunting, you need to be as unobtrusive as possible. Use cover and shadows to hide your silhouette and always hunt into the wind. Actually, I'm not as worried about my airborne scent as I am what I leave on the ground. Whitetails, especially older deer, will remember where they encounter human scent and you can burn an area even after you're left it. So I wear rubber boots and will frequently put some fox or coon urine on the soles to hide my scent trail. And I'm careful not to touch branches or brush up against limbs or brush."

Terrain and deer sign dictate the pace of Bill's hunts. "If I'm not seeing what I want, I'll book right through an area until I see deer sign," he says. "But if I'm into deer, I'll just creep along. Sometimes in an entire evening's hunt I may only go a couple hundred yards. Your best advantage is to see the deer before they see you, and to do that you have to be moving slowly."

Naturally, camouflage helps Bill close the gap on ground-level whitetails. "I always wear camo, but I'm not a slave to fashion," he quips. "I frequently mix up patterns to break up my outline; Realtree top, Mossy Oak pants, whatever. The rule of thumb I use is to wear camo pants to match the forest floor, and a jacket to match the vegetation or tree colors above. Once it cools down, a pair of dark wool pants topped with a camo jacket works really well. If there's snow on the ground, I may wear white pants and a camo top."

Wearing camo and using natural cover to break up your silhouette are essential for still-hunting success with a bow. (Bill Vaznis photo)

Top-quality optics are also essential for the still-hunter, Bill says. "I'll go back to the vehicle if I forget my binoculars. If I'm going slowly through a good area, all I may see is just a part of a bedded deer. Binoculars let me check it out and identify it. I was stalking the edge of a cornfield once and I spotted this fuzzy-looking brown thing. I dismissed it at first, but as I looked for other deer, my eyes kept coming back to it.

"Finally I looked through my binocs at it, and it was the ear of a really nice buck, looking right at me. Once he saw I was looking at him he was out of there, but if I'd spotted him just a little earlier. . . . All I know is, I live by my binocs; they not only help me spot deer, but sign. I can look at a tree from fifty yards and determine if it's got a rub on it and the size. That can save you a lot of walking in the course of a day."

Bill's willingness to "think outside the box" has proven that bowhunters can adapt to pressured deer, provided they're willing to adapt their strategy and adopt techniques that are out of the mainstream.

SPECIAL SITUATIONS

Opportunities for most whitetail hunters are, at best, either holding their own or declining somewhat. But archers, who can pursue whitetails in areas where firearms aren't allowed, are often seeing an expansion in both the number and variety of places they can hunt. And this can mean a shot at deer that aren't pressured as hard as they are in other areas.

Two factors are at work here. First, there is increasing awareness of the effectiveness of archery tackle by biologists and game managers. Second, whenever bowhunters have been given a chance to "do the right thing" to manage a whitetail herd, they've

When scouting opportunities and hunting time are limited, studying topo maps to identify likely deer travel routes and cover is invaluable. (Bill Vaznis photo)

usually responded right on cue. The happy result is an increase in hunting opportunities, not to mention the incredibly positive PR we gain from such hunts.

While there are many such "special" hunts, there are two common scenarios. One is a limited-entry, short-duration hunt in an area normally off limits to hunting: state, county, and/or city parks; preserves; and military installations. There also are extended hunts allowed by municipalities and suburbs experiencing whitetail damage problems. Because of the unique challenges inherent in these hunts, bowhunters must be particularly careful to hunt safely and ethically and act as ambassadors for all sportsmen while pursuing whitetails.

Suburban/metro hunts are discussed in detail in chapter 8, so let's examine the first type of special hunt. Since my home state of Minnesota has such a hunt, I'll relate the experiences of several friends who've participated.

The Camp Ripley hunt is held over two weekends in late October each fall. Bowhunters who are drawn participate in only one of the three-day hunts. Archers must check in at the main gate each morning, then proceed to their hunting area. No pre-scouting is allowed. At the end of each day, bowhunters must again check out, so hunt organizers are assured no one is lost or injured.

Though the area is quite large, several hundred archers participate in each weekend hunt. And because they have only three days, many bowhunters still-hunt or make small drives to each other, hoping to score without waiting for a buck to walk past their treestands. Ripley veterans say that whitetails are either bedded tight or on the move, the latter a result of either hunter activity or the impending rut.

How does a bowhunter score in such a situation? By applying some of the scouting tips covered in chapter 3. My friend Mike Rain, who's hunted Ripley several times, prepared by first studying topo maps of the area and identifying funnels and travel corridors he felt bucks would use.

Ripley is a combination of rolling hardwoods, swamps and lowlands, and small openings. Such cover is ideal for funneling whitetails as they move between patches of cover. As we've learned from previous hunters, deer *can* maneuver through anything if they have to. But where they *will* travel when moving naturally or under moderate pressure is fairly predictable.

Studying topo maps allowed Mike to identify several likely travel corridors for hanging a stand. But that wasn't the only function of the topo. Because pressured deer were being pushed by other hunters, they frequently bedded down and held tight. With only a couple of days to hunt, Mike and his two friends decided that waiting for deer needn't be their only option. So they made small "pushes" to drive deer to each other.

While driving is a technique most associated with gun hunting, Mike proved that bowhunters can pull it off by harvesting a fine mature buck on a Ripley hunt. The keys to executing pushes with a bow are (1) tackle only small chunks of cover, (2) move slowly, and (3) use the wind to your advantage. Drivers (or perhaps "pushers" is a better term) should slide into position with as little disturbance as possible. Walk slowly—even still-hunt—toward the agreed-upon starting place.

Standers need to take similar precautions, with a caveat; they can't allow their scent to blow toward known or suspected bedding areas. Remember, the goal of a push is simply to nudge deer in a direction they'll already want to go. And they certainly won't head toward an area where they've smelled danger.

When drivers and standers are in place, the "push" begins. The drivers should move slowly; no whooping or hollering, just an easy-going pace designed to alert—not alarm—deer. Since driver numbers are small, and the men are moving slowly, alerted white-tails should simply rise and trot off, rather than hightailing it to parts unknown. Remember, standers are shooting with slow, limited-range weapons, so running shots at distant deer aren't an option.

Standers need to set up on the downwind side of escape trails. They should keep some type of cover at their back (a shoulder-width tree, clump of brush, overturned tree root, etc.) that will camouflage their silhouette but still allow them to shoot. Facemasks or paint are recommended, as the human visage is easily spotted by ground-level deer.

Finally, standers should strive to stop any deer that are moving, with a low whistle, grunt, or bleat. Unless you've practiced extensively at moving targets—and most of us haven't—you're more likely to make a lethal shot at a motionless or slowly walking animal.

Using this technique has yielded deer for many hunters at Ripley and during similar short-duration special hunts. It is not, of course, for every situation. If hunter numbers are dense, or if the hunt area is a sensitive one (a park near an urban or metro area or a state park where non-hunters may be present), do not bother pushing deer. Stick with stand hunting in proven or suspected travel corridors and wait for close-range, slam-dunk opportunities at stationary deer.

In such situations, the image of all bowhunters is far more important than the biggest whitetail such a place may hold.

FINAL THOUGHTS

Bowhunting is not normally an activity associated with pressured whitetails. Indeed, most successful archers will tell you that they go out of their way to hunt deer that are experiencing as little pressure as possible. Yet, as bowhunter numbers continue to rise, and the normal areas available to us shrink (or simply change thanks to development and habitat loss), the number of archers encountering pressured whitetails is likely to rise.

Thankfully, the examples of the hunters above remind us that we can still be consistently successful at taking good bucks and at finding new hunting opportunities.

And remember that there is an issue involved that's even more important than tagging deer. As we face more and more situations where the public encounters bowhunters—during urban or other "metro" hunts on small tracts of land owned by commuters, retirees, or other non-farmers—it's imperative that we adopt the highest standards of personal behavior and ethics. Though our hunting brethren and a growing number of biologists recognize the importance of our sport in managing deer herds, there are vast numbers of people who remain uneducated. To bring such people into our camp—even if they never participate in the sport—is essential.

If we all serve as energetic, forthright, and positive examples of safe, ethical hunting—despite the increasing pressure of competition for whitetails in areas accessible to large numbers of hunters—we can act as ambassadors for a sport that should remain vital for many decades to come.

7

DRIVING
TECHNIQUES

We simply called it "the swamp drive." My family's central Wisconsin property has a lot of low ground on it, but everyone knows what you're talking about when you say "the swamp," especially if you add the adjective "big."

The Big Swamp runs for nearly a mile and is owned by one Bestul or another for over half that distance. Unlike some swamps, ours has wonderful variety, with lovely stands of tamarack, small pockets of treeless marsh, dense alder thickets, and little copses of spruce. A clear creek flows along one side, hinting at the volume of water that lies just beneath the muck most everywhere else.

Like many swamps, it is infested with whitetails at certain times of the year. Naturally, we were most concerned with the November firearms deer season, especially the seven days following opening weekend. After being bumped, harassed, and shot at in the hardwoods and popple thickets for two days, our whitetails retreated to the Big Swamp. There, in the boggy tangle of reeds and grass, brush and timber, they could relax and lower their blood pressure—at least until we decided there were no more deer in the easy places to hunt, which is when we would decide to get our feet wet.

I don't know when my family first started making the swamp drive, but it was already a tradition when I began hunting in 1972. For a twelve-year-old, there is nothing quite as exciting as a deer drive. The larger the maneuver, the more I liked it. I was not only assigned the simple-but-pleasing man's work of pushing bush, but I was encouraged to perform slightly crazy behavior like hollering, whistling, and breaking all the brush I wanted. All the rules of deer hunting from a stand were pitched into the fireplace, and there's nothing an adolescent loves more than anarchy.

The Big Swamp ran roughly east to west, with the creek a meandering border on the north side. We invariably pushed the cover from the west, sliding six—and sometimes as many as ten—drivers along a lake edge to begin. We'd try to line up so we could see each other, which was an easy task near the lake where trees were either dead or widely spaced.

But that visibility was quickly lost in the first 150 yards, when we hit tag alders and other dense cover. Once in the thick stuff we hollered the ubiquitous "Ho!" every so often or simply called out the adjacent driver's name in an attempt to keep a straight line. Some standers were posted at creek crossings or on escape trails into the highland timber on the swamp's north edge. But the greatest commitment of ordnance went to the road bordering the east side.

Some of these posters were actually members of our hunting party. I never quite figured out how the word spread, but every year hunters whom we'd never met would drive for miles around to join in. While most were just innocent onlookers, there were always a fair number of brazen folk who'd post confidently along the road to try and pop a deer or two. Besides the obvious trespass and safety violations these ne'er-do-wells committed, I was struck most by their rudeness. Not only were they crashing our party, none of them ever offered to drive.

But as a youngster back in the brush, I rarely had to deal with such worries. Like my fellow swamp-stompers, my world was divided into two simple activities: not getting lost and keeping deer from slipping between me and the guys on my right and left. Accomplishing these goals was simple in kinder terrain, but in the swamp it became the equivalent of juggling chainsaws; focus on one task for a moment too long and the other was ready to bite you.

I could relate several tales of the lost-hunter variety, but the most vivid remains a middle-aged woman who decided to make a small "push" through a particularly dense section of the swamp, hoping to drive a buck to her waiting husband and sons. After slogging about for a while, the woman realized she was lost. She panicked and started to run. Her progress was halted when she stepped into one of the swamp's many sinkholes, black, fetid, nearly bottomless quagmires. The woman thrashed in the hole for a time, but only worked herself in deeper. Finally, alerted by her frantic yelling, her boys came to pull her out, the muck up to her armpits when they arrived. The sinkhole sucked the insulated boots off the woman's feet during the extrication and nearly got her shotgun, too.

Back to the deer. They could be impossible in that place. There were few mature bucks around back then, but the ones we had were scary-smart and any of their under-aged brothers that had survived opening weekend were catching on fast. But the old does, especially a mature nag leading her fawns, held advanced degrees in escape-ology. They bobbed when we weaved, ducked when we ran, and showed us just how serious a deer can be about staying alive when all signs indicate otherwise.

It was on the swamp drive that I first learned how desperately pressured deer want to double back through the drivers—and how frequently they accomplish that maneuver. One year my cousin Stuart, who was about my age, was assigned to drive along the creek, a particularly thick and swampy route. I was next to him. As we approached the last 150 yards of the drive, a section choked by tag alders and willow brush, we slowed our pace to a crawl. We could hear deer milling in the cover ahead. Finally a large doe, her three fawns, and a trailing doe broke and trotted back toward Stuart and the creek. My cousin focused on the lagging doe, as her pace offered the best chance for a shot.

Momma and the triplets snaked through the alders, crossed the creek, and popped into the open timber forty yards away on the other side. Expecting his doe to follow, Stuart aimed at the distant creek bank and waited. He flicked his safety off as he watched the doe plunge into the creek, waiting for her to clamber up the opposite bank. Nothing.

Figuring the doe was standing in the water and would eventually get nervous and break, Stuart waited. No deer. So he crept to within what would have been bow range of the bank. He could hear water dripping from the deer's belly into the creek. More waiting. More dripping. My cousin, athletic and a good hunter, crept even closer. The dripping stopped. Still no deer.

Finally, unable to take the suspense, he walked confidently to the creek, determined to at least bust the doe from her midstream position. But she had vanished. "I think she turned into an otter and swam out," Stuart laughed as we resumed the drive. We have always wanted to know what trick Ms. Houdini pulled to execute her amazing escape.

I was in my mid-twenties when we stopped driving the Big Swamp. Though we'd killed many deer in this tangle, it was an event that had run its course. We began to lose hunters to age, disinterest, and other forms of attrition. Safety concerns were a factor, as well; it was always a huge drive and the potential for accidents—especially with the inevitable outsiders—was high. And as we became interested in growing some mature bucks, we backed off driving in general, not wanting to push our yearling bucks to parts unknown. The Big Swamp was a natural refuge, and we decided to let the deer pour in there if they wanted to.

Still, I will always recall that drive, and the many smaller ones we executed, with fondness. Driving is an outstanding method for harvesting deer that are simply not going to move by any other means. It is also a tactic that works wonders if you

Drives can still net trophy-caliber bucks, even in areas where hunting pressure is intense.

don't have time to wait for natural movement, or where conditions hamper the feeding or rutting patterns that put deer on their feet. Driving is also an excellent tool for covers and habitats that are difficult, if not impossible, to hunt by any other method.

There's another important facet to driving whitetails that goes beyond simply flushing and harvesting deer. By studying the response of deer to carefully applied pressure, you can gain a better understanding of how they utilize their habitat; bedding areas are revealed, travel routes become evident, and little-known security covers are uncovered. Simply put, if you drive deer on a property—even if it's only a time or two—you can often learn more about their use of that property than you could in years of stand hunting.

Let's take a look at this ageless but ever-exciting method and how modern hunters can employ it not only to harvest pressured deer, but also understand them better.

MINI-DRIVES:
LOW IMPACT, HIGH SUCCESS

It was the next-to-last day of the New York firearms season when Charlie Alsheimer got the call. Alsheimer, a world-class whitetail hunter, photographer, and writer, listened intently to his friend Paul Daniels's plan.

"He told me to head for a stand I'd hung in a good bedding area prior to the season," Charlie remembers. "Then, when he got off work about 2:30, he'd make a still-hunt in the area and see if he could get a buck on its feet."

Charlie slipped into position at 1:30, sneaking along a slim walking trail he'd prepared when he hung the stand. As he crawled up the tree trunk and settled in, Charlie's hopes were high. Not only did he respect his buddy's hunting ability, he knew that Paul was going to execute a "clover leaf still-hunt," a tactic the pair had used in the past with great success.

"The clover leaf is a quiet, low-impact method of moving deer that doesn't make them bust out of an area," Charlie explains. "It works basically like this: The stander heads to a spot within a known bedding area. I prefer to have a stand hung there, with a walking trail made that will allow a silent entry. The stander should get in position well before the other hunter starts his route.

"Then a lone still-hunter proceeds to make big, slow loops toward the stand hunter. Each time he gets almost within sight of the stand, he meanders away from his partner. Once he's made a complete loop, he shifts slightly over and repeats the process until he's made four big loops that encircle the stand. Terrain, cover, and the size of the bedding area dictate how large the loops are, but in my mostly wooded hunting area, they average about three hundred yards. Viewed from above, these loops resemble a four-leaf clover, with the stand hunter positioned directly in the middle."

Charlie notes that the walking hunter often gets shooting on this drive, depending on his skill as a still-hunter. "Paul is an ex-

Clover Leaf Still-Hunt

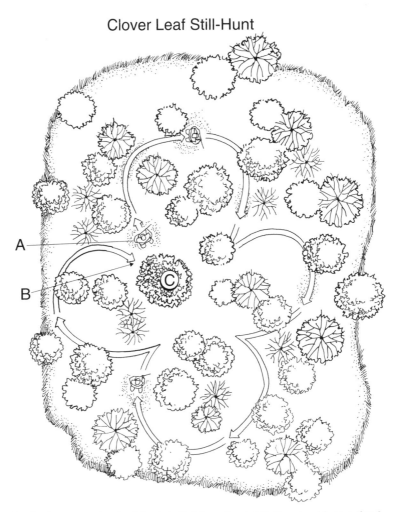

Hunter begins hunt at point A, ultimately finishes at point B. Treestand is at point C.

cellent example," he says. "He is a very skilled deer hunter and has killed several bucks while doing his loops, which he prefers to sitting in the stand. Though he walks with the intent of pushing deer for me, Paul is always on the lookout for deer and ready to capitalize on an opportunity. On many of these still-hunts Paul will complete the entire clover leaf and I'll never see or hear him."

That was the case on the day Charlie received his call from Paul. "I'd been sitting since 1:30, and about 4:00 I could hear a deer coming," Charlie remembers. "The buck came at a fast walk out of a deep ravine, paused at the top and looked down his backtrail. I knew Paul was down there somewhere, though I hadn't seen or heard him. After the buck relaxed, he trotted toward me and I was able to kill him nearly within bow range.

"That 8-point was the largest buck I'd ever killed on the property with a gun. After I shot, sure enough Paul came walking up and said, 'Well, how big is he?' and I said, 'He's pretty nice.' Paul was making the third cloverleaf when he jumped the buck."

According to Charlie, the beauty of this tactic—besides the fact that it can be executed with only two hunters—is that it doesn't panic deer. "The idea is to get a buck up on his feet and walking, not busting through cover. There isn't the noise and confusion of larger drives; the deer are just concerned with avoiding that one man moving slowly through the woods. That makes their movements more slow and circular. They're reluctant to leave that security cover, which frequently gives the stand hunter an excellent shot at them as they move. I've told many people about this tactic and have heard from them that it's been successful in a variety of habitats."

Charlie employs another small-drive strategy he calls the "two-man still-hunt." Another low-impact tactic, this method is

Two-Man Still-Hunt

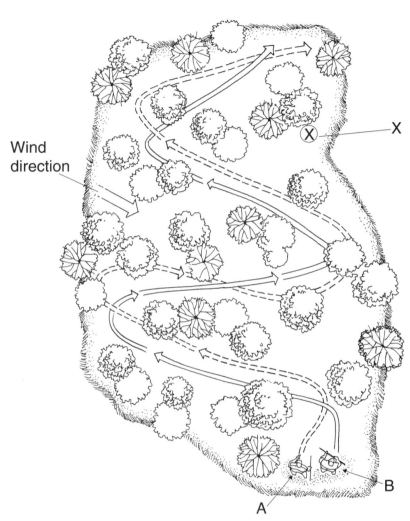

Wind
direction

X

Hunter A follows path indicated by dotted lines; hunter B follows path indicated by straight lines. Treestand is marked by X.

designed for a pair of hunters, but could easily incorporate a third, as a recent hunt Charlie enjoyed illustrates.

"I'd been seeing a really nice buck, an 8-point in the 140-class, on our property before the season," Charlie recalls. "But I hunted the entire bow season and never saw him, and the early part of the shotgun season didn't produce, either. I was beginning to wonder if he had been shot or maybe moved off the property. But I knew if he was still around he was moving mostly at night, which is common behavior for mature bucks."

The gun season was well underway when Charlie received another phone call from hunting buddies. "They told me they wanted to do the two-man still-hunt in a section of woods, and advised me to get in a nearby stand," he recalls. "So once again, I managed to slip into a pre-hung stand in the hunting area."

At an agreed-upon time, Charlie's friends began their hunt. "It begins with the first hunter entering a bedding area (or other security cover) moving into, or across, the wind," he says. "After the first hunter has walked some distance, usually 75 to 150 yards, the second hunter begins, walking either directly in the first hunter's tracks or slightly off to one side. They move slowly, with the intent of seeing deer before they are seen and getting a shot. The difference, of course, is that if the lead hunter bumps a deer, the second hunter is behind him. Since a common behavior of an alerted whitetail is to circle, the second hunter often gets shooting at a deer spooked by the lead man."

On this day, Charlie's friends had another trick up their woolen sleeves: a third man, sitting in a treestand some four hundred yards distant. "I began seeing deer from my stand as the hunt progressed," Charlie remembers. "Some were nervous, but others were moving about very at ease." Indeed, one of these calm deer was a buck Charlie knew well—the big 8-point he thought had disappeared.

"He was actually trying to breed a young doe shortly after I first spotted him," Charlie says. "So he was clearly not spooked.

In fact, when I finally shot him he was within easy bow range. I suspect that he was bedded near that doe and when she got up— either alerted by the still-hunters or another deer they had bumped—he rose to follow her. I'm convinced I'd have never seen, much less shot, that deer without the tactic."

Charlie prefers these low-impact "drives" because they pressure deer but don't send them running off the property on high alert. Charlie is a devout advocate and ardent practitioner of Quality Deer Management principles, and he has no interest in passing on young bucks, only to spook them to neighboring properties where they might be vulnerable to harvest.

Yet regardless of how carefully he hunts his property, Charlie has to deal with the fact that whitetails experience some degree of pressure, especially during popular firearms seasons. Small pushes like the ones just described can help hunters harvest deer under similar conditions. They are also an outstanding option when small parties are looking for ways to move deer to each other.

UPPING THE ANTE: MAKING LARGER DRIVES WORK

I remember, when I was a teenager, reading an article in a hunting magazine about driving deer. Since this was a tactic I adored, I read the article with relish and nodded my head in agreement when the writer said that a well-organized drive is one of the most efficient, practical methods for harvesting whitetails. I fairly ran to my father to share this line, but was amazed when he only chuckled. Was he mocking the writer or the method of hunting I'd grown to love?

"Neither," Dad said. "But that sentence hangs on the words 'well organized.' That's the toughest part of the whole deal and sometimes we're just not." I was somewhat crestfallen, as Dad clearly didn't think of our party as the well-oiled machine I did. But as I grew older I realized the honesty of his statement. Sure, we often *moved* deer on just about any push we executed. But *killing* them by having the drivers and standers work in perfect unison? That was a tall order, even on drives we'd been doing for years.

No one knows this better than my friend Pat Reeve, an expert whitetailer and former guide. While the bulk of Pat's guiding duty was to put mature bucks in the lap of waiting stand hunters, driving was a big part of his job when he worked for veteran outfitter Tom Indrebo.

"After the opening weekend of the gun season, most of the mature bucks were holding tight to some kind of cover and not moving," Pat says. "If we wanted our clients to score, we had to push deer to them."

When driving whitetails is part of your vocation, you learn your lessons in a hurry. Pat realized the necessity of matching the number of available hunters with the cover to be hunted, as well as to the rhythm of the drive itself. "Basically, you can divide drives into two kinds," Pat says. "One is a drive where you're trying to nudge deer to the standers, the second is when you deliberately try to panic whitetails into moving. Usually, the choice you make depends on how well you think you can cover the terrain."

With a moderate to large number of drivers, Pat feels the nudging approach is often the best. "If you know you have enough people to really cover things well, the drivers can take their time and work through everything. We liked to line drivers up so they could see each other and try to maintain that spacing. From the many drives I've done, I believe bucks have one of two personalities; they're either edgy, nervous deer that want to immediately run from cover, or they're thinking deer that analyze a drive and figure out how to beat it. Those thinkers are the ones that want to double back through the drive or hold so tight you walk by them."

Pat feels deer that double back do so because they sense a gap in the line of drivers. Maintaining visual contact lets drivers foil such attempts because it allows them to keep a relatively straight line as the drive progresses. Any sags or breaks in the line simply provide a buck with the opening he needs to slip through. "Actually, one really effective way to get your drivers shooting, and often fool a thinking buck, is to fake a gap in the line," Pat says. "Sometimes we'd have a driver or two who would remain as silent as possible while the others made some noise as they walked. Bucks would sense a gap there and try to run through it. I shot a really nice 8-point as a driver using this tactic once. The key is to make sure the silent drivers have a quiet path to walk, like an old logging road, field edge, or grassy opening."

To boot up the skulking deer that behave like rabbits, drivers have to investigate every available piece of cover. "It's hard to underestimate how tight a buck can hold, and in what seems like no cover," Pat says. "You need to walk up to every brushpile, blowdown, tangle of vines, or ditch you see. One of my friends was about to walk past a rusted-out vehicle lying in the woods when he stopped for a second near it. A buck actually came bombing out of that car's windshield. Walk slowly, stop and pause, and zigzag. A steadily walking hunter following a straight line makes it easy for a buck to lay there and let him walk by."

How will whitetails react when pushed from security cover? Groups that enjoy the most success know the answer to this before they even set foot in the woods. (Pat Reeve photo)

With a large number of drivers, just "nudging" deer ahead of the line often works best. (Pat Reeve photo)

Minus an effective number of drivers, Pat says that a small group can sometimes accomplish big results if they cover territory in a different manner. "If I know I'm too short on drivers to fool those thinking bucks, I do the opposite of slow and methodical. I want to create a panic, an immediate threat, that disorients the deer and just makes them react and run. I don't want to give them time to think or analyze. I want them on their feet and moving right now."

To create such hysteria, drivers enter the woods noisily and at a quick pace, going out of their way to create a ruckus. "They can smack branches against tree trunks, yell, or even use noisemakers like a whistle," Pat says. "There's something about a whistle that really panics a whitetail. If you're working hilly country or ditches, the drivers can toss rocks and sticks downhill. This not only makes a lot of noise, it makes it seem like there are more drivers than are actually there."

Despite the din, this approach can often move a mature buck, Pat says. "A lot of these deer have seen drives all their lives and know they don't want any part of one. So often their first reaction to a bunch of guys entering the woods is to immediately bust out of there."

Also, Pat notes, if whitetails are stacked in the cover to be driven, getting the first deer on its feet and fleeing will often create a chain reaction among other deer. "Sometimes that big, mature buck is the first one out of the drive and hauling the mail. On other drives he may be the last deer out of the woods, right on the heels of the others. Your standers have to be alert, because the deer they see are often coming pretty fast."

Naturally, bush-pushers are only half the equation on any deer drive, and the best drive-masters pay equal attention to where standers are placed and how and when they get there. "One of the toughest jobs when I was guiding was to get standers to understand the drive," Pat stresses. "Before each drive we'd pull out a topo map or aerial photo and explain exactly where everyone would sit, how the drive would progress, and what we expected the deer to do. We'd synchronize everyone's watches and predict how long things would take, so standers wouldn't become worried they were left behind and leave their spot. You'd be amazed how many times a driver would come through and not find a man where we'd set him.

"We really stressed getting standers in place silently and long before the drive began, even if we had to walk them to the spot.

Since it was often cold, we made sure they had clothing to hang in there and not freeze out. And it's important to match the hunter with the spot you put him in. Some guys can't hear very well, so you put them where they're more likely to see deer coming. Or if a guy couldn't walk well, he got the place closer to the road. You try to make the best fit of the hunter's ability to the demands of the setup."

Since driven whitetails are obviously alert to danger and often moving quickly, standers must position themselves to remain hidden, yet shoot effectively. "I always like to put a gun hunter with more cover at his back and less in front," Pat says. "On archery drives it's the opposite; you want to have a little screen of brush in front of you to hide your draw. Scrape out the leaves and snow in a circle around you so you can turn your feet or make a small move without making noise. As soon as you see deer, anticipate their path and make any adjustments slowly.

"When a deer is in range but moving, I like to stop it with a low whistle or grunt. You'll usually have to make it fairly loud, as the deer is running, listening to his own feet in the leaves or snow and his breathing. If he doesn't stop when you whistle, he doesn't hear you. And wait for the deer to be broadside for the most lethal shot angle. Too many guys get excited and want to shoot as soon as they see deer. Let them come if they're coming and stop them for that broadside shot."

Using these techniques, Pat has enjoyed consistent success over the years, often taking bucks that had eluded his stand setups. "One memorable buck was a 10-point we called 'Tilter' because of the way his rack leaned," he recalls. "Tom and I had videotaped Tilter many times over a two-year period, and we

When the drivers really let loose with a lot of noise, deer bolt for new cover.

knew right where he lived. Unfortunately, we were never able to kill him from a treestand, despite many attempts.

Finally, during the latter part of gun season, we decided to make a drive through his bedding area. Sure enough, Tilter busted out of the drive early and hauled the mail across a nearby field. But we had a stander posted on the far edge of that field, and Tilter ran right up to him for an easy shot. I don't think we'd have taken that buck any other way."

UNDERSTANDING ESCAPE ROUTES: THE KEY TO SUCCESSFUL DRIVING

While the general goal of driving deer—getting them to move in the direction of waiting standers—is obvious, the specifics of actually putting those deer in shooting range of standers is an art form rarely understood or practiced. Even the most bungled drive can produce excitement in the form of white-tails flagging through the woods, but to consistently put nice bucks on the meat pole requires a sophisticated knowledge of how deer escape the pressure of approaching hunters.

I've met few people who understand this concept better than my good friend Ted Marum, who guides whitetail hunters in the country's number one county for producing Boone & Crockett bucks. Buffalo County, Wisconsin, is not only rugged, hilly, beautiful country, it is arguably some of the most difficult terrain to hunt in the nation. Though the area is heavily farmed, there are blocks of timber so large and hard to access that they rival tracts of Big Woods. The steep hills present not only challenging topography, but the requisite hurdles of fickle winds and frustrating thermals.

Standers should be comfortably situated to take the best advantage offered by the terrain and their hunting skills. (Pat Reeve photo)

Many a hunter has noted Buffalo's impressive tally of B&C entries and visited the region, intent on tagging a monster. But most leave deerless and frustrated. This area has been Ted's classroom for many years, though, and he's proven himself an adept student of big-buck escape patterns.

Ted's knowledge is based on gathering a deceptively simple base of information. "Basically, I want to identify security covers—places that bucks feel safe—and how they reach those covers," he explains. "Until you know those two things, it's very difficult to drive deer with any degree of success. Big bucks in particular rarely go anywhere by accident, even during the heat of a drive. If you can predict those places ahead of time, you have a chance of killing them. If not, you're relying on luck or just catching a deer in a place where he's vulnerable."

According to Ted, one of the first steps in deciphering buck movements is the simple, but oft-neglected, art of observation. "Whenever I see a buck somewhere, whether it's in a hunting situation or just while I'm driving down the road, I immediately ask myself, 'Why is he there?'" he says. "It's rarely a coincidence that a buck walks where he walks; he's there for a purpose. He's feeding or traveling from bed to feed (or vice versa) or running somewhere to escape pressure. When you see him doing that, he's giving you a glimpse into his world; where he feels safe. Put enough of that information together and you can kill him. And don't rely just on your own experience. Any time I hunt new property I ask the landowners where they frequently see deer. Those patterns usually repeat themselves."

Often, a long-distance observation will reveal a general behavior, but more specifics may be needed to kill the deer. "For

Identifying escape trails is one key to putting standers in the right places.

example, you can see a nice buck heading for a thicket, but can't see exactly where he enters it," Ted says. "Then you can walk to that general area and read the sign to see specifically how he uses that terrain. Rubs and trails will usually be there to help you fine-tune your understanding."

Naturally, some of this information will be gathered in other hunting or scouting situations and some during drives. "Generally, the behavior of bucks during a drive is specific to the terrain and will be repeated by deer for years," Ted says. "That's why it's so important to observe where deer run when they're pushed. If you can pinpoint the general way they move through the landscape, you won't notice a big variation in that for years, unless some drastic change in the land—logging, a new house, etc.—occurs."

Ted has noted several general escape patterns in the hill country of Buffalo County that he has seen repeated in other habitats he's hunted. "As a rule, a pressured buck will usually try to gain elevation from danger," he says. "So it's typical for them to work their way up a ridge where they can see, and usually hear and smell, better. Plus, most pressure comes from valley bottoms in hill country, and getting higher than hunters just gives a buck more escape options."

While bucks will frequently gravitate toward a ridgetop for these reasons, they rarely travel the spine of that ridge when being driven. "They're more visible there and they know it," Ted stresses. "A ridge-running buck is often a dead one. So they'll drop off to one side and travel along the sidehill where there's often a band of dense cover, usually on the south side of the slope. And, of course, they'll use any terrain features to hide

Veteran bucks sometimes seem to just melt away when pressured during a drive, even when faced with a stretch of open ground.

themselves as they travel. They'll cross the ridge through a saddle or swale or dip, rather than busting across the top."

As a buck attempts to exit the driven cover, it will use similar terrain features to remain hidden, Ted says. "Our drives usually end at a field, and you'd assume killing a buck would be easy once he popped out in the open. But it's amazing how they can cross open country and use any little low spot to escape. Once you've identified those crossings, they'll remain consistent. We make one drive along a huge timbered ridge that, when it ends, is surrounded on three sides by fields. Out of hundreds of possible options, any big buck on that drive will come out in one of two little swales. One of the last times we made the drive, a buddy of mine killed a 10-point with a 19-inch spread. Shot him at twenty steps, coming down one of those swales."

The natural tendency for most hunters making drives is to place standers along escape routes and adjacent to the cover being driven. While Ted says this tactic can be successful, he's learned a better way. "The biggest problem with posting tight to the cover is that most of your shooting will be at deer moving Mach One. But if you've studied your deer and know where they'll wind up when they escape the drive, why not put the stander there? Anywhere in fragmented cover—like farm country, for example—bucks will bust out of the woodlot you're driving and immediately head to a patch of distant cover—another woodlot, a creek bottom, a field of CRP. Since there's usually a field separating the two, they'll have the burners on going across the field. But as soon as they hit that next patch, they'll usually stop and either immediately relax or look back at the drive. If your stander is sitting there, he has a shot at a standing deer, often at point-blank range."

If the escape cover is off the property you can hunt, Ted suggests setting a stander along the escape route, but as far off the cover being driven as possible. "Here again, your knowledge of how deer move between those two covers is important," he says. "They may travel through a weedy ditch, or along a brushy fencerow, or just beat it for a little clump of trees or a power pole surrounded by grass in the middle of an open field. Any stander set along these escape routes will usually have a lot better shooting than if he was tight to the drive."

Regardless of the terrain, knowledge of escape routes is an invaluable tool when driving deer. Identify the avenues that pressured deer take to safety and your chances of success are high; guess at them, and your attempts to harvest bucks will be hit-and-miss . . . and usually more of the latter.

SAFETY CONSIDERATIONS FOR DRIVING

There may be no other hunting tactic where safety is as important as it is when driving. For starters, there are simply more people concentrated in a smaller area than there are for other methods. Second, all those hunters are frequently on the same level, and the bullets they fire are traveling parallel to the ground. Finally, the deer are often moving quickly, which can cause a hunter to focus more intently on his target than on what's around or beyond it. In the excitement of a drive, the rules of safe gun handling and hunter conduct can often be put on the back burner, sometimes with tragic results.

Keep safety paramount in every hunter's mind on a deer drive. Plan carefully, making every party member aware of where posters are situated and where drivers will come through. Take a few seconds before each push to remind everyone that

Hunters who stick to safe, well-crafted drive plans will enjoy themselves more and see more tangible results.

the prime purpose of the drive is not to kill deer but to be safe so they can hunt another day.

If you see another hunter engaging in unsafe behavior, correct him or her with a gentle but firm reminder. If you instill a "safety mindset" in your group—a conscious commitment to proper weapons handling and correct shooting behavior—they'll be less likely to get caught up in the heat of the moment and commit a serious error.

Even in areas where it's not required, wear blaze-orange clothing on your torso and head. Avoid deer-colored clothing containing shades of brown or white. If you're pushing thick cover where visibility is limited, maintain constant contact with other drivers by talking or whistling softly. When deer are sighted, make your first thought, "Where are the other hunters?" instead of "When can I shoot?"

I noted earlier that one of the reasons we abandoned our Big Swamp drives was out of a concern for safety. This was largely due to the hunters who were not members of our party. It was also on that annual push that, while our line of drivers approached the standers, I once had three slugs whistle through the treetops over my head. They did not come that close to me, but they came close enough. I never figured out who the shooter was, and that is exactly the point. I didn't know where he was and he certainly (I hope) didn't know my position.

There is no room for such doubt when you are handling firearms. Driving is an enjoyable and rewarding tactic, but to do it right requires a total commitment to safety and ethical hunting practices. Anything less is simply not enough.

8

THE SUBURBAN/METRO CHALLENGE

The buck stood thirty-five yards from the centerline of a busy highway. He was staring blankly ahead, his giant rack tipped slightly forward, the rays of rosy, late-afternoon November sunlight bouncing off heavy beams and tines so long they appeared artificial—like a kid had drawn them with a pair of huge white and pink crayons. It remains the largest whitetail I have ever seen, and he was standing no more than ten miles from downtown Minneapolis.

As I mentioned earlier, I live in Minnesota, a state that has produced its share of trophy-class whitetails. Some of these giant deer live near my home in the rural, southeastern corner of the state. And I've been lucky enough to harvest a few of these Gopher State monsters. So I've seen some awe-inspiring antlers.

But that buck, which seemed planted in the middle of that highway cloverleaf, was something special. Not only was he an awesome example of what a whitetail could be, he stood blissfully unaware of the hundreds of cars zipping past him. I'd like to think he made it across the exit ramp and into the safety of the woodlot on the other side. Heck, I'd like to think he's still alive, living out his days in a city park and wowing folks with that incredible headgear.

That deer wasn't the first hint I'd had at the tremendous deer-hunting potential of metro areas. Over the years I've had several friends who've enjoyed fantastic success on "civilized" whitetails. One buddy has a wall full of shoulder mounts from suburban bucks, another has played cat-and-mouse with a world-class metro wallhanger for years, and a cousin (who shall remain nameless) had the buck of a lifetime staring him in the face on a hunt in a county park not long ago.

Unfortunately, my cousin was sleeping at the base of his stand tree at the time, exhausted from a week's work. He woke up to find the buck ogling him from just ten steps. And, of course, there was nothing he could do but watch the deer of his dreams trot away. It's still unclear who scared whom the most during that brief encounter.

For hunters seeking new opportunities away from the intense pressure of public wildlife areas, suburban whitetail hunting may be the answer. But while it's well known that whitetails have adapted beautifully to suburbia, gaining permission to hunt these often-abundant herds can be a tall challenge. With habitat small, fragmented, and invariably privately owned, access to the limited pockets of cover is difficult and competition can be fierce. Add to that hurdle the fact that most landowners are either non-hunters or antihunters, and the chances of denial are pretty high. Anytime I need a reminder of the prevailing sentiment toward hunters in urban areas, I can reflect back to the very first whitetail I killed, referred to in the Introduction to this book.

As I mentioned, I was twelve at the time and my world was a simple one. I had divided it neatly into two groups of people: deer hunters and those who supported us. And I believed this analysis without doubt. After all, it was a perfect reflection of my family and all the families I knew. Those who did not hunt at least understood why others wanted to hunt.

I got a harsh introduction to the real world as my father and I drove home from that opening weekend hunt. It was Sunday night and we were tooling slowly through the streets of Madison, a college town that hosts the University of Wisconsin. The year was 1972, not long after the vocal, passionate, and sometimes-violent protests against the Vietnam War that took place at "the U-Dubya," as it was often called.

As the law required, we had tied my buck on top of the trunk of our Dodge sedan; displaying harvested deer—at least in this instance—wasn't done for bragging rights, it was DNR policy. But the pair of women who pulled up next to us as we waited for a stoplight thought otherwise.

Dad and I were talking quietly to each other, likely reliving some exciting aspect of the hunt, when I heard a horrific screaming. Since our windows were closed, I didn't immediately identify the source, but in my peripheral vision I noticed the driver of the adjacent car gesturing wildly at us. I rolled down my window and turned to face the woman, thinking she might be in need of help.

Of course, it was *she* who thought *we* needed some guidance. I still don't recall every word the woman and her partner screamed at us that cold November night. But none of it was kind, and their language was full of epithets; some were phrases banned from our household for years, others I'd never even heard before. My father, a religious, kind, and soft-spoken man who had never uttered a curse in my presence, chose wisely not to respond and did his best to distract me from the tirade. But before the light changed and we lost the shrieking women, I got the proverbial earful. My introduction to the world of antihunters was both swift and unforgettable.

That my short course in Animal Rights 101 took place in a big city is not, of course, a coincidence. As our cities continue to grow, gobbling up farmland, rural dwellings, and small towns, the base of people with a vital connection to Nature—and an understanding of hunting—has shrunk proportionately. This trend has been covered in great detail in other writings, and I see no need to reexamine it here. But the point of this chapter is to address a simple, yet vital irony: With the dense whitetail populations found in much of urban/suburban America, hunters may be needed more there than they are anywhere else. Yet in these same areas—also densely populated by people— hunters are undoubtedly understood the least.

Perhaps no one realizes the implications of this situation better than Rob Lucas, who lives in Norwalk, Connecticut. Rob, a family man and successful physician's assistant, has been on a personal crusade to demonstrate the effectiveness of using hunters to manage whitetail herds in suburban areas. In his wealthy home area, situated only a stone's throw from New York City, whitetails have exploded into every available wrinkle of habitat. As in many suburbs, those wrinkles are largely composed of parks, golf courses, and small, privately owned woodlots.

Deer damage in the form of vehicle collisions, overbrowsing of habitat, and the spread of disease is significant and much discussion has occurred about the best management options to control whitetail numbers. Rob has been a one-man wrecking crew intent on showing the public that hunters are the best solution (particularly bowhunters, as firearms discharge is banned in this and many other urban areas).

Whitetails have adapted well to civilized areas. But as their populations have increased, new hunting opportunities have been created in places that put the management of deer herds at odds with antihunting groups. (Rob Lucas photo)

A FOOT IN THE DOOR

Like many deer hunters living in suburbia, Rob knew the potential role that sportsmen could play in this unique habitat. But he also knew that a large percentage of the public, including property owners, often didn't share that knowledge. Interestingly, a series of related incidents now have Rob facing a unique challenge; having the time to visit all the properties he has permission to hunt.

"When I first started trying to hunt here in 1989, access was difficult, without a doubt," Rob admits. "But three things have lined up to change that. The first is the growing number of municipalities that have been forced to deal with the deer problems that result from unchecked herd growth. They've looked at a variety of solutions—everything from sharpshooters to contraceptives—and in many cases realized that bowhunters are the most efficient, cost-effective method.

"The second situation was the rising toll of deer damage in the area. As deer are forced into smaller and smaller pieces of fragmented habitat bisected by roads, there's an inevitable spike in the number of deer/car collisions. This happens regularly here in the spring and fall, when whitetails are most active. You don't have to go very far to find someone who's hit a deer with a vehicle, and some people have had multiple accidents. Add to that the damage that browsing deer do to trees, shrubs, and other plant species, and public tolerance for whitetails was simply wearing thin.

"The third, and perhaps most important, factor was the growing occurrence of Lyme disease in the area. [This tick-borne illness actually gained its name for the nearby town of Lyme,

Connecticut, where it was first discovered.] In a recent survey, up to 40 percent of the households in certain areas had had at least one incidence of Lyme disease in the family. Since Lyme disease can be debilitating, and in some cases deadly, especially to the very young and very old, people were realizing that the whitetail population had gotten completely out of control."

While Rob credits these external factors for creating the right environment for hunters to get a toehold, it was his impassioned response to another situation—the rising voice and disagreeable behavior of antihunting groups—that created a unique opportunity. "There are three major animal rights groups in the area and whenever there was a discussion of whitetail management in the local newspapers, they'd respond with passionate

Suburban landowners have had to deal with a variety of problems related to burgeoning whitetail populations, including the overbrowsing of expensive landscape plants and the threat of Lyme disease. (Rob Lucas photo)

letters against hunting or any lethal control," Rob says. "So I decided that someone—make that someone who understood hunting—needed to respond to those letters."

And Rob did just that, voicing his own opinion in a public forum—with a hunter's viewpoint. But instead of resorting to the name-calling and emotionalism that antihunters so often lean on, Rob went out of his way to remain dispassionate and rely on factual data to support his case. "Basically, I just shined a bright flashlight on the hypocrisy of these groups," he says. "I'd just pick apart their letters and respond very calmly and coolly to each belief they held or accusation they made. I'd cite scientific studies, like the one examining the small percentage of wounding loss at Camp Ripley in Minnesota. I'd illustrate how, if left unchecked, a whitetail population could explode in just a few short seasons. I'd quote Leopold, Ted Kerasote, or Dr. Dave Samuel. I'd write a very pointed letter, but one supported by facts. And then I'd sign my name and include my address and telephone number."

Even Rob was amazed by the response to his letter campaign. Landowners experiencing deer damage would call him up and *ask him* to hunt their properties. When he visited someone with a good-looking section of woods in their backyard, the landowner would often recognize Rob's name and realize he was a serious, thoughtful, and responsible sportsman. "When I visited a new place, I'd introduce myself, talk to the owner, and leave them a packet of information about me," he says. "That packet includes a business card, a copy of my hunting license and bowhunter safety certificate [Rob is an instructor], consent/permission forms for the landowner, and an agreement that absolves

By working hard to convince landowners that careful, responsible hunting can work in populated areas, Rob Lucas has been able to take some nice bucks. (Rob Lucas photo)

the owner of any liability if I, or another hunter with me, is hurt while hunting their land."

Such attention to detail—and his responsible behavior while afield—has only made Rob's list of properties grow. "Actually, one of the first things I try to do is enroll the landowner as my agent," he muses. "I tell them that I can be much more effective as a hunter if I can connect as many properties together as possible; in other words, if I keep hunting property X and the deer move next door, it's more difficult for me to harvest one unless I can also hunt property Y just down the road. So I ask landowners to tell their neighbors about me, which is an invaluable tool. If I show up at your door and you don't know me, you're going to be naturally suspicious. But if your neighbor makes the introduction, I have an excellent chance of getting in."

And like all ethical hunters, Rob does his best to nurture and maintain the relationships he establishes. "Every landowner is different, of course," he says. "Some don't want to know when I come and go. They give me permission and then basically don't care to know I'm around. But others want me to check in before every hunt so that they'll know what to say if a neighbor calls to tell them there's a stranger in their woods. There are even some landowners who are simply interested in what I'm doing and how the season is going, to the point that they want an update on the 'body count' as the season progresses. You have to understand each property owner's expectations and wishes and respect them to maintain that access."

Perhaps the most important element of Rob's success is that, well, he's successful. The reason he receives permission to hunt properties is because he harvests deer and helps control the population. While there are mature bucks in suburbia, and no one likes tagging them more than Rob, he focuses on his task as a herd manager and concentrates his harvest on antlerless deer.

"Last season I shot thirty-four does, the season before sixteen, and the season before that a dozen [as in many metro areas, Rob can receive unlimited antlerless tags]," he says. "That's the way I earn my keep in this country. If I were in farmland, I'd help the farmer with chores he needs done—baling hay, picking rock, fixing fence, whatever. The favor I can do for these people is to shoot their deer. That's why they want me here and I try to perform."

To reduce the overall number of deer in an area, Rob first harvests as many does as possible. (Rob Lucas photo)

Naturally, Rob and his family can't eat that much venison in a year, but he has that base covered, too. "We've helped set up a donation program to give venison to local food shelves and needy families," he says. "We even have a butcher who processes the meat at a reasonable fee. He also hauls a walk-in rental cooler to a central location so when we [Rob hunts with several friends] shoot a doe we can field dress it and haul it to the locker. Every couple of days the butcher comes by and checks the cooler. I even encourage my landowners to pay for the processing of these donated deer and many of them do. It's a program that's become popular in the community, and shows just another contribution hunters can make."

Such a high-profile approach might seem out of touch—if not downright dangerous—in such a setting, yet Rob says just the opposite is true. "I keep expecting to get threatening letters from the antis and it just hasn't happened. And the response of landowners has really been positive. Just last fall I was getting ready to head out for an evening hunt and had parked my car along a cul-de-sac. I was pulling my camo on when I heard someone yell at me. I turned to see a little old lady standing on her porch and braced myself. But she just hollered 'Are you that Rob Lucas guy?' When I said yes and explained that I was going out to hunt on her neighbor's place, she just smiled and yelled back 'Good. Well, go get 'em.'"

MAKING IT HAPPEN

While whitetails may be abundant in suburbia, don't think for a minute that these deer are pushovers. Once a human steps from a backyard and into the woods, civilized whitetails morph from placid browsers to wary, highly pressured deer. "They definitely know the difference between Mr. Jones heading out to his garden and me," Rob chuckles. "Leaving human scent and making repeated visits to an area really shakes them up. So I work very hard at practicing low-impact hunting, getting into and back out of areas quickly and quietly, then resting them. By doing that I've kept my stand sites productive. In fact, I have some stands where I average taking a doe once every two hunts."

Unlike less fragmented habitat such as vast woodlands or farms, suburban hunting spots require minimal scouting, according to Rob. "You can actually do quite a bit without leaving your vehicle. I hunt for at least a part of the day for some sixty days each year, but if I'm late getting home from work and can't hunt,

Successful suburban hunting often boils down to placing a treestand in exactly the right spot in a small woodlot.

I'll drive around and look for animals on the move. I've also had great luck with some landowners; I ask them if they're seeing deer to call me, especially if they're noting any kind of pattern. Then when they call, I make the effort to get over there and hunt. That not only lets the landowner know I'm helping control his deer, it keeps him involved in the process.

"As far as on-the-ground scouting, I don't bother looking for food sources, because food is literally everywhere. There are some pretty traditional bedding areas and I stay completely out of them. So I focus on funnels and travel corridors that connect blocks of cover; a strip of woods between a golf course and a waste treatment plant, the dense cover surrounding a pond in a housing development. Since the covers are so small, you can often spot these funnels from the road, and when you visit them the trails are usually easy to identify. The trick then is to pick the right stand site and be smart enough to not overhunt it. Frequently, I'm hunting little woodlots no more than an acre or two, and there's one spot in there for a stand. If you keep coming back, you'll burn it out."

Once a stand site is picked, a new challenge presents itself. "Getting to a stand without alerting deer here is very difficult, because they're frequently bedded very close by," Rob says. "In fact, it's not unusual for me to look up and see a big doe watching me as I walk in. When that happens, I try to act very nonchalant, like I'm just out gardening and I'm looking for my lost hedge trimmer. I may even talk to myself quietly and move tangentially to the deer, avoiding direct eye contact. Frequently that's enough for the deer to relax and move off slowly. It's important to not have her blow out of there, because she'll alert other deer and your hunt will be over for that night."

After tagging numerous does, Rob and his hunting partners are able to tackle the challenge of taking big bucks. (Rob Lucas photo)

Often, deer are bedded nearby but out of sight, ready to spook just at the sound of Rob's approach. "I used to clip a little walking trail so I could get into my stand quietly, but that blew up in my face," Rob laughs. "The deer would use it too, so they'd wind up walking right at me, smelling my scent trail and going on high alert. So I've had to get creative; I may run or trot into my stand, or bunny-hop, or skip. Anything to not sound like a two-legged predator. I tried grunting on the way in, but of course that pulled a buck that was bedded nearby right in before I was ready. Another good trick is to have a partner walk in with you, then walk back out. That's usually all the deer need; they heard a human come in, then leave, so they relax. Fortunately, they can't count by the sound of people in the leaves."

Rob has numerous examples of the sophistication of Connecticut's suburban whitetails. "There are some very old does here, and they often come through the woods, looking for danger in the treetops. And of course, bucks too; on one early-fall hunt, I had a bachelor group of four bucks come in. There was a spike in the lead, followed by a 6-point, then a good 8-point, with a real dandy in the rear. Well, they walked across my entry trail and the spike didn't flinch, but the middle bucks started milling around and acting nervous. And I wear Scent-Lok clothing and rubber boots. That's all the warning the big one needed. He stopped and stared for the longest time. Finally, though he never knew what the other bucks were nervous about, he just turned to leave. Fortunately for me, he was still well within bow range when he did that. I had a perfect, quartering-away shot, which I made."

As in all habitats, suburban whitetails travel largely in doe family groups, and Rob makes every effort to harvest the large "alpha" doe. "If you get a group of does and fawns to come in and

Fooling older does is always tricky—even in areas where they're used to seeing quite a few humans. (Rob Lucas photo)

can only shoot a small one, it's better than nothing, of course," Rob says. "But hunting those deer the rest of the season will be very difficult. In fact, you might not see them on that property again for the rest of the fall. But if you can take the lead doe, you've just set yourself up for some very good hunting. Without her guidance, the rest of the deer just aren't as wary. And once that alpha doe is gone, the herd is disoriented; they don't know who's in charge anymore, and they move about more freely. Then your chance of harvesting the other deer goes way up."

Rob has used other strategies to adapt to wary urban white-tails. "I've started hunting more from ground blinds," he says. "Especially in areas where good stand trees are hard to find. In the right situation, small pushes can work very well, especially if you've observed the escape behavior of deer in that particular cover. They'll repeat the same behaviors—stop by the same fence, jump over a stone wall in the same spot—over and over. Oh, and I'm always on the alert as I walk in to my stand. I've taken a good number of deer that were just watching me walk in; I just pretended to ignore them, but kept looking for a shot. If they present a shot and I know I can make it, I take it. Again, being able to pull that off is all in your approach and demeanor; you're not trying to catch a plane, so you might as well hunt your way into the stand."

A WHITETAIL HUNTER'S LEGACY

Although the majority of whitetailers will continue to pursue deer in less civilized habitats, it's likely that hunting opportunities in suburban/metro areas will increase in scope and size. On a large scale, this is due to a growing awareness among municipalities—and, indeed, state game departments—of the ability of hunters to manage deer herds.

On a small scale, opportunities will expand if all hunters behave like Rob Lucas; demonstrating on an individual, daily basis that sportsmen are law-abiding, ethical, and committed to the very tenet we've used to justify our existence for decades—that hunters play a vital role as a natural predator in any ecosystem.

"The fact that I harvest does and help control the herd growth is, I believe, more responsible than any other factor for the hunting opportunity I enjoy," Rob says. "If you're not killing does, you're not helping landowners with their problem. Traditionally, the harvest composition in Connecticut has been about 50/50 [bucks vs. does]. I hope in the future we'll tip that figure heavily toward antlerless deer. In some of the areas that I hunt, a harvest ratio of four does for every buck is the bottom line to check herd growth.

"Shooting does is something concrete that hunters can do to give back to the resource, to become a participant in Nature's cycle. When we go out and pass up a bunch of over-populated does to harvest an immature, 6-point buck, it's the ultimate form of 'taking' in my book. You know, one of the most common tactics of the animal rights groups is to portray hunters as 'clients' of the game departments; that they main-tain deer herds at high levels so that we can enjoy our 'blood sport.' We can battle that kind of rhetoric by proving that we can do what is necessary by keeping the herd in check."

It's often said that society consists of a small percentage of hunters, an equally small percentage of antihunters, and a re-maining majority that are simply non-hunters who may have their opinion swayed by either group. That truism certainly exists in Rob Lucas's world, and he does his level best to sway public opinion. "Many hunters are too intimidated to approach the owner of a million-dollar estate and ask for permission to hunt," he says. "But I've been amazed at the reception I've received. There is no doubt that people enjoy having deer around. But as the popula-tion escalates, the tolerance goes down. One landowner I ap-proached illustrates this attitude perfectly. He liked having deer in the area, but he was eager to have me hunt. His response when I asked for permission was simply, 'Go ahead. It's been a long time since deer have been cute in this neighborhood.' "

Perhaps of greatest interest to other hopeful metro-area hunters, Rob feels strongly that his experience is not unique and could—make that should—be repeated by other hunters. "There is absolutely no reason that I should be the only hunter enjoying this opportunity," he stresses. "In fact, my philosophy has always been that the more of us who participate in this sport, the better. I do my best to help my friends and other ethical, serious hunters to have an opportunity. It's what we do with that opportunity that will decide whether we keep it or lose it.

"When I'm out there, I behave all the time as if someone is watching me which, as Aldo Leopold wrote, is the definition of ethics. But while I certainly have a lot to lose by doing wrong—I'm becoming locally well known as a hunter, instructor, editorial writer—I [hunt properly] because it's the right thing to do. It feels good to hunt this way. Being politically active is my way of giving back to the sport that's meant so much to me, of ensuring that hunting will be there for my son when he grows up. There are a lot of indicators that say it might not be, but I'm going to do everything I can to preserve the hunter's role as a part of Nature."

TAKING IT TO THE STREETS

While Rob Lucas is a stellar example of what hunters can accomplish in metro areas he is, of course, just one man operating in one small piece of turf. There is a growing list of cities, suburbs, and other civilized areas with burgeoning deer populations. Likewise, there are countless hunters living in these areas who'd like nothing better than to have quality hunting close to home. Yet many deer hunters view hunting in suburbia as just as daunting a prospect as finding whitetails in a wilderness area. Thankfully, there are places to get help in hunting this new frontier.

There are already several state game departments that have established special hunting units in metro areas. Ohio, Pennsylvania, and Indiana—to name just a few— all host such hunts. In my home state of Minnesota, special urban hunts are a vital part

Hunters willing to adapt to the realities of hunting around urban areas can score on some nice bucks, but it takes a commitment to hunting ethically and safely at all times.

of the deer season and are widely participated in. In the Twin Cities (Minneapolis/St. Paul) area, the Metro Bowhunters Resource Base (MBRB) is a group that was formed just to help the DNR and municipalities with such special hunts. The MBRB not only works with cities to examine their deer problem and suggest possible hunting solutions, they also supply the hunters.

To qualify for such hunts, the MBRB requires that a hunter first become a member, then take a certified bowhunter education course, pass a proficiency test, and sign an agreement to abide by the hunt rules. Frequently, there will be special training/orientation sessions unique to each hunt, and they must be attended by all participants.

Such a commitment assures community leaders that participating hunters are not only qualified, but serious. MBRB's success has led to the establishment of a growing number of annual hunts held in several suburbs. They are a powerful and proactive voice for game management in the greater metro area and serve as an example for other bowhunting/sporting groups to follow.

What can you do if no such group exists in your area? Contact the local game manager and inquire about special-hunt opportunities for individuals. If none exist, consider getting a local archery club or sportsman's organization involved to help lobby for them. Attend city council meetings when deer management is on the agenda and ask to speak on the topic. Rest assured that any animal rights groups in the area will be present and demanding to be heard. The only way to combat their rhetoric is to counter it with the truths of modern game management and the many examples of how hunters have succeeded. Speak in polite, reasoned tones and don't be baited by antihunters. Cities are looking for reasonable, cost-effective solutions for their deer problems; suggest the cheapest, most efficient method going.

As the example of Rob Lucas illustrates, the conduct of hunters in suburban units must be impeccable for those opportunities to continue. Not only must whitetailers obey the letter of the law, they must observe the highest ethical standards. Marginal shots at deer must be passed on at all times, with the hunter striving for only close-range, high-percentage opportunities. Blood trails must be followed diligently and whitetails recovered quickly and transported to a vehicle unobtrusively.

I know one suburban deer hunter who shot a fine buck on a hunt a few years ago. The shortest drag back to his vehicle was a route that would skirt the backyards of several homes. Instead of

While few hunters are as organized and determined as Rob Lucas in seeking access, being able to take bucks closer to home should be good motivation for making the effort.

this easy route, the hunter chose a more difficult, circuitous path that avoided dwellings. He later won an Ethical Deer Hunter Award from a state hunting organization.

After participating in such a hunt, follow up with your success stories and feedback. Rob Lucas produces a newsletter that he distributes to landowners at the end of each hunting season. In it he details how many deer were harvested and where, points to the potential herd expansion he controlled, and suggests possible improvements for upcoming seasons. "For example, our hunting season used to close at the end of December," Rob says. "I pointed out to landowners that we could be even more effective if we had another month. We lobbied for a season extension and, with the help of area residents, received it. The year after that happened, I pointed out in my year-end newsletter that twenty-five percent of the deer I killed were in the month of January. People had a visible result for their efforts."

Metro-area hunting may not appeal to every whitetailer. Many of us pursue solitude and scenery as much as we do game, and the suburbs pale in comparison to the prairies of Kansas or the mountains of Kentucky. But there are plenty of whitetails living closer to home, and for modern hunters dealing with the realities of chasing pressured deer in hard-hunted areas, these suburban whitetails might just prove to be a bonanza.

THE FUTURE: ADOPTING A PRESSURED DEER ETHIC

I was in my early twenties when I shot a whitetail that had been wounded by another hunter. I had already filled my buck tag that cold November morning, but when the small-racked 6-point limped into view, I knew that I should finish it off. Group bagging was legal, and there were two members of our party within earshot who would tag the buck. Besides, shooting the deer seemed the right thing to do; staring through my binoculars, I could see the slug had entered the buck's front shoulder and exited through the brisket. While I've seen deer survive traumatic injury and recover, my gut told me this one didn't stand much of a chance. So when the buck hobbled on three legs to within thirty yards of my treestand, I aimed behind his shoulder and fired. The whitetail slumped, almost gratefully it seemed, into the snow.

Within thirty minutes I could see a trio of hunters approaching, following the buck's blood trail. One was my cousin Scott, the other two apparently the men who'd wounded the buck. I hailed Scott and pointed toward the fallen deer. Once my cousin saw the dead whitetail, he walked over to hear my story. As I related the morning's events, I kept glancing over Scott's shoulder at the two men, who were gesturing at the deer and talking excitedly. Finally, I saw one reach into his pocket and fish out a tag.

"Are those guys tagging that deer?" I asked Scott.

"They better not be," he said as he turned to walk toward them. I climbed down from my treestand and followed. By the time we reached the men, they were indeed about to tag the little buck. My cousin, not a man to mince words, stopped them in the process and a heated discussion followed. It was the classic who-should-get-the-deer scenario we've all read about or experienced. The trailing hunters claimed the buck was theirs because they'd drawn first blood. Eventually, they claimed, they'd have caught up to the buck and finished him off.

While I respected their story, I had my own. "I realize you hit the buck, but my shot killed it," I said. "Yes, the deer was limping and may have eventually died, but you could have tracked him all day and never found him. I appreciate your effort, but your shot wasn't fatal and mine was." The two men were clearly irritated by my analysis and at one point even claimed that my double-lung bullet hole was theirs. Since they'd tracked the buck over a half mile already, I think even they knew they were grasping at straws.

My cousin interjected a third opinion. "As far as I'm concerned, you guys are trespassing right now. I should be taking your license numbers and calling the sheriff." He had a point, as well. Under state law, hunters needed to make every reasonable effort to retrieve wounded game, but if the animal crossed into private property, the hunter was required to contact the landowner and receive permission before proceeding. If the landowner denied access, the tracking stopped at the property line.

So who was right? We all were, at least to a degree. And, as in any argument, righteousness was fanning the anger we all felt. I could see the frustration building in the eyes of the trailing hunters. The veins in one man's forehead were pulsing, and he was flexing his hands like a boxer preparing for a match. My cousin was equally rigid. This was his land, and he trusted my story implicitly—and he had been battling trespassers for years, including some who claimed to be trailing deer. That these men actually were was beside the point. It seemed a line had been drawn in the snow and someone was about to cross it.

I don't know why it took so long for it to occur to me, but suddenly a thought popped into my head that was as clear as the sky was cold. "It's only a deer," the thought said. "It is not something worth fighting over with two men you don't even know." Of course, the thought was supported by something that no one knew but me; I already had a buck down and tagged. I had only shot the wounded buck out of pity. If it had come walking through on its own, in fine shape, I'd have likely let him pass. It was this sudden realization that prompted me to blurt out a sentence that probably averted a fistfight.

"You can take the deer," I said. My cousin, who is my best friend and someone who reads me well, looked at me like I'd just wrapped my own arm behind my back and yelled 'Uncle!' The trailers were similarly dumbfounded, but relaxed visibly. "I mean, why don't we split it?"

"What?" the trailers asked, nearly in unison.

"You take the deer now," I offered. "Get it butchered and you can have half the meat. I'll take what you don't want to eat and the rack." Even during diplomatic discussions, you can't separate a buck hunter from his horns. I had a five-gallon pail full of dinky antlers from bucks like that one at home, but I couldn't bear to see the headgear go.

The men smiled. Hands were shaken. A time and location for dropping off my half of the deer was appointed. The trailers tagged the buck, looped a rope around its antlers, and leaned into the long drag out to the road. As it would turn out, that's the last time I ever saw that buck. Scott and I ran into one of the men several days later, and he claimed the deer had been stolen off their car as they'd sipped beer at a local tavern. Of course, we didn't believe the story, and I was angry for a long time after whenever I thought of their deceit. But time has allowed me to chuckle over that tale. It was, of course, just a deer. Not something worth a deep-woods brawl or even a long-standing grudge. To this day, I'm glad that I let the men have the buck.

I tell this story not to say that I, or any of us standing over that little buck in the snow, had a lock on Truth or The Right Way that morning. I tell it because I think of that day quite often, especially when I'm sharing the woods with other deer hunters.

It's a situation that's becoming more common, as it seems we're all being forced into smaller territories. Land is sold and permission is lost. Another hunter gains permission on "our farm." Housing developments and urban sprawl eat up once-prime hunting ground. Wealthy folks buy up farms and either restrict hunting to a few individuals or shut it down completely. Public lands become crowded. Weary of the hurdles presented by difficult access, some whitetailers simply drop out of the sport.

But those of us who remain have a responsibility to each other. We can compete for access to prime ground or the hot stand site or even a big deer, but we need to respect each other in the process.

The easiest thing in the world is to see those "other guys" in camo or blaze orange as competition when, in fact, they are comrades. We have much more in common than we have to argue

As hunting pressures continues to rise, our conduct among other hunters becomes even more important. (Pat Reeve photo)

about and, ultimately, how we treat each other is going to speak as loudly about our sport as the first crack of a rifle on opening morning.

It's important to note that I am no Pollyanna. I am fully aware that there are rude, boorish, and idiotic people in the deer woods. There are also stand-stealers, habitual poachers, and any number of opportunistic scofflaws. I'm not suggesting that we tolerate crass behavior or ignore violations of ethics or the law. We should correct hunters who make errors in judgment. We should turn in those who break the game codes. Every time we avert our eyes and ignore a hunter who behaves improperly or illegally, the reputations of all sportsmen suffer in the process.

But to the hunters who do behave properly—the ones who conduct themselves like gentlemen, uphold the regulations, and respect the whitetails we all cherish—we owe a measure of tolerance, even admiration. In an ideal world, we'd all have a thousand acres of prime whitetail habitat to roam at will. But we live in a quickly evolving society, and it's one that's going to force us all to share.

Let me share another example. Not long ago, I received permission to hunt a wonderful farm close to my home. The property is a wildlife haven, full of turkeys, small game, and some truly giant bucks. In my first two seasons on this property, I saw more mature whitetails than in the previous eight years of hard hunting on a variety of other farms. I would love nothing more than to have the exclusive run of this real estate, and I'm confident I could tag a good deer every year there if I did.

But there is a wrench in the works, and it's a wonderful one. The landowner is a fine gentleman, concerned not only about wildlife, but about providing opportunity for hunters. Robert hunts himself and has many friends who share his love for the sport. So Robert divides his farm into sections, or sets aside seasons, and we each take our shot in the limited real estate or time frame we're allotted. There are understood boundaries and gentlemen's agreements and we all get along—and appreciate to a man the privilege we share. In these days of high-priced hunting and limited opportunity, a small slice of the pie is better than no dessert at all.

Last spring while shed hunting (the one activity for which I'm granted free rein on this farm) I found some absolutely dead-nut, killer stand spots that no other hunter was using or aware of. Naturally, they are not on the chunk of ground I've been able to bowhunt. Each time I found such a setup, I stood there for a long

Respecting the rights of other hunters won't prevent you from bringing home bucks like this one.

time, picking a stand tree, planning an entry and exit, and deciding on the proper wind direction and timing for hunting there. And then I walked away. The places are burned in my mind, and as I write this I'm anxious to share them with the hunter lucky enough to draw that area. I'd love nothing better than to see one of the other guys—or, even better, Robert himself—shoot a monster deer from "my" spots. That's the spirit of cooperation and acceptance that the landowner has established and fostered, and I'm privileged to be a part of it.

We live in a highly competitive world these days. Jobs, money, status, belongings—it's natural to strive for such things and, consciously or not, compare our personal success with the success of those around us. Having been an athlete from middle school through college, I believe competition is healthy. Without setting goals, and then striving to reach those goals, we become complacent, smug, and eventually, lazy. All successful people— deer hunters included—are continually working to improve on past success.

But I'm just as firmly convinced that competition can get out of control and lead to frustration, anxiety, and even distaste for the very pursuit we once loved. I've seen many deer hunters— including some close personal friends—take their desire for success in our sport to this extreme. Initially, they set difficult, yet attainable, goals and work hard to achieve them. Then the bar is raised higher and higher, until they reach a nearly inevitable point where competition is replaced by obsession. Many times these people are not even aware they've crossed a line. Sometimes they are, and I've known several who have stopped deer hunting because they recognized, and were repulsed by, their extreme desires. I view such dropouts as tragedies.

So what are reasonable goals for the modern deer hunter sharing the woods with others? There is no specific answer that fits us all. But I do believe there are some guiding principles. First and foremost, we need to remember that deer hunting is supposed to be fun. For the vast majority of us, hunting is recreation. We don't need it for sustenance and, with a few rare exceptions, it's not going to make us wealthy. If your devotion is so intense that hunting is no longer the enjoyable sport it once was, perhaps you could be setting your goals too high.

Second, hunting "right" means observing all game laws and the highest ethical standards. If you find yourself tempted to bend a rule (or ethical standard) or probe its "gray area," it should be a warning sign.

There are hundreds of examples of ethical misdeeds that could be listed here, of course. But I'd rather rely on the simple definition offered earlier by Rob Lucas: Behave at all times like someone is watching you.

A final tenet involves our attitude toward, and treatment of, other hunters. It's an important issue, because our attitudes influence our behavior, and there has been no other time in the history of hunting when sportsmen need each other like we do now. Do you greet other hunters at parking lots or when you meet them in the woods? Inquire about their luck or offer help in dragging out their deer? Congratulate them when they've bagged a trophy and offer to take a photo? I've been fortunate enough to be on the receiving end of such calculated acts of kindness and the effect is always the same. They not only make my day, they make me feel connected to something larger than myself. It's the same feeling I enjoyed when my father shook my hand over that first buck so many years ago.

The future of deer hunting lies in passing on a strong hunting ethic to the next generation.

We've covered a lot of ground in this book. We've examined the unique adaptations whitetails make to avoid hunting pressure. Seen some of the innovative techniques hunters employ in response and some of the alternatives to hunting in highly pressured areas. And heard stories of success and tales of woe.

In the process, we've met some people who can offer more than tips and tactics for dealing with pressured whitetails. They stand as examples of how a person should conduct himself when the woods are crowded with other people who share a similar passion. They are Deer Hunters, and I'm proud to be one of them.

INDEX

A

Access, 204, 227
Active field, 75
Adaptations
  to hunting pressure, 14
Aerial photos, 150
  importance of, 65–66
Alsheimer, Charlie, 175–180
Antihunters, 202, 205–206
Archery drives, 186. *See also*
      Bowhunting
Areas
  bowhunting, 157
Attitude
  toward other hunters, 231

B

Bedding, 63
  areas, 91, 99, 114
    hunting, 102
    scouting for, 157–158
  patterns, 36
Behavior
  and science research, 32
  breeding
    mature bucks, 45–46
  crass, 228
  natural
    learned survival
      mechanism, 35
  stop-and-stare, 83–84

Behavior (*cont.*)
  survival
    fawn, 44
  unsafe
    correcting, 196
Benches
  travel areas, 42
Bernier, R.G. "Dick," 118,
    129–136
  still hunting, 122–128
Bestul Book, 12
Bice, Ron, 76, 78, 80
Big bucks
  photo, 213
Big Swamp, 169, 170
Binoculars, 75
  essential for still-hunter, 162
  use of, 12, 13
    scouting, 72
Biologists
  capture whitetails for
    telemetry studies, 30
Blaze-orange clothing, 196
Blood trails, 220
Boone & Crockett bucks, 188
Boots, 137
Bowhunting
  aggressively, 153–154
  areas, 157
  experiences, 115–118
  first kill experience, 141–144
  from ground, 154–162
  pressured deer, 144–147
    personal experience, 20
  public areas, 145, 147
  special- or limited-entry
    hunts, 145
  stalking, 156

stalking example, 153–154
Stan Potts experiences, 147
suburban hunting
    opportunities, 145
  tactics, 141–167
    driving, 165–166
    pushers, 165–166
    scouting, 165
    still-hunting, 159
    still-hunts, 157
Breeding behaviors
  mature bucks, 45–46
Bucks, 135
  big bucks
    photo, 213
  Boone & Crockett, 188
  eluding pursuit, 133
  mature. *See* Mature bucks
  movement per day, 48
  personalities, 182
  ridge-running, 192
  shed
    clue to identifying core
      area, 70
  signs, 124–125
  tracks, 131
  trophy-caliber
    drives, 174
  urban
    photo, 219
  use grassy cover, 49
  veteran, 193
    melt away, 193
  vs. does
    tracking, 130
Buffalo County, Wisconsin,
    188
Bush-pushers, 185

C

Cameras, 78
  and scouting, 78
  multiple setups, 80
  positioning, 78–79
  remote
    to discover deer, 76
  remote-sensing, 77
Camouflage
  for still-hunting success, 161
Camouflage gear, 160
Camouflage pants, 160
Camouflaged deer, 125
Camp Ripley hunt, 164
Chamois shirt, 137
Climbing stands, 106
Clothing
  blaze-orange, 196
  camouflage, 160
    for still-hunting success, 161
  camouflage gear, 160
  camouflage pants, 160
  chamois shirt, 137
  ensemble, 110
  layering, 110
  list, 110
  Mossy Oaks pants, 160
  Scent-Lok, 214
  still hunters, 136–139
  wool, 137
Clover leaf still hunt, 175–180
Clues, 125
Competition, 227, 230
Conduct, 227
Confidence, 152
Cooperation, 230
Cover, 212
  escape, 63

  description, 98
  security, 94
Crass behavior, 228
Creekbeds
  travel areas, 42
Crossings, 194

D

Danger
  elevation from, 192
Daniels, Paul, 175–180
Daypack, 110
Deer
  ability to avoid intrusions
    within home range, 29–46
  able to elude dogs, 50
  adaptations
    to civilized areas, 203
    to hunting pressure, 14
  behavior
    and science research, 32
    stop-and-stare, 83–84
  characteristics, 56
  damage by, 204
  eating patterns, 36
  environmental adaptation, 16
  getting on their level, 124
  habitat
    looking for, 61
  migratory
    in refuge, 43
  movement, 90–94
    and science research, 32
    deciphering, 190
    pattern midday, 35
    per day, 47
    response to hounds, 50

Deer (*cont.*)
    response to human
      presence, 37
    shift timing, 34
    time of day, 153
    one that got away, 51–54,
      83–86
    in your own backyard, 53–56
    patterns, 134
      establishing, 73
      shifting, 34–38
    population, 6
    pushed from security cover,
      183
    refuge
      migrating *vs.* sedentary,
        43–44
    response to hounds, 48–51
      movement distance, 50
    responses to predators, 34
    revealed, 63
    sedentary
      in refuge, 43
    senses changing
      according to hunting
        season, 21
    shift movements
      response to human
        presence, 37
    shift patterns
      adjust to human pressure, 38
    signs
      importance of, 160
    suburban
      sophistication, 214
    summer
      observing, 75
    travel areas, 42
    understanding, 14

Deer hunter's paradise, 17
Deer Ridge Wildlife Area in
    Lewis County, 46
Deer-funneling terrain, 67
Does
    family groups, 214–215
    harvesting, 209
    lead, 215
    older
      fooling, 215
    radio-collared, 39
    vs. bucks
      tracking, 130
Donation program
    venison, 209
Dougherty, Craig, 95–98
Dougherty, Neil, 95–98
Drivers
    bowhunting tactics, 165–166
    creating hysteria, 184–185
    pressured deer
      doubling back through
        drivers, 172–173
    techniques, 169–197
Drives, 18
    archery, 186
    habitat utilization, 174
    large, 180–188
      organization, 181
    safety, 195–197
    small, 175–180
    swamp, 169, 170
    trophy-caliber bucks, 174

E
Eating patterns, 36
Elevation
    from danger, 192

Entry points, 75
  notes for journal, 75
Environmental situations
  causing pattern shift, 37
Escape cover, 63
  description, 98
Escape patterns, 192
Escape routes, 188–195
Escape trails, 166
  identification, 191
  leads to security cover, 97
Establishing sanctuaries, 94–
    99
  definition, 94–95
  management strategy, 95
Estrous scent, 78
Ethical standards, 220, 231
  pressured deer
    adoption, 223–233
  violations, 228
Everyman's trophy, 6

F
Facemasks, 166
Family groups
  doe, 214–215
Fawn
  survival behavior, 44
Feeding areas, 63
  observing, 74
  scouting for, 157–158
Feeding-type trails, 90
Firearm season
  personal experience
    pressure deer, 21
Firearms, 137
Firing line effect, 45

First deer hunt, 1–3
Food plots
  sanctuary, 99
Fortitude, 114
Frustration, 230
Funnels, 212
Future, 223–233

G
Game codes, 228
Game laws, 231
Game plan
  develops, 150
  for hunting, 149
Gear. *See also* Clothing
  camouflage, 160
  list, 110
  still hunters, 136–139
Glassing, 12, 13, 152
  need for, 56
Going for broke, 99
GPS
  using to establish patterns,
    73
Ground blinds, 108, 215–216
  portability, 108
Ground-bound
  hunting, 156
Ground-pounders, 120
Growth
  unchecked, 204

H
Habitat
  looking for, 61
Habitat utilization
  drives, 174

Hang-on type stands, 104
Herd
  keeping in check, 217
Herd growth
  unchecked, 204
Home range, 44, 47
Homework, 25
Humans
  as predators, 15
Hunters
  adaptations to pressured deer,
    14
    personal experience, 10–
    13
  attitude toward, 231
  attitude toward others, 231
  conduct, 226–227
  crass behavior, 228
  deciphering patterns, 24
  fellowship, 2
  learning from science, 51–
    52
  lost
    tales about, 171–172
  pheasant, 39
  treatment of, 231
  viewpoint, 206
Hunting
  adjusting for other hunters,
    145–146
  aggressively, 118–121
  arrival and departure time,
    102
  early years, 1–3, 5
  low-impact, 210
  pressured whitetails, 14
  sport *vs.* way of life, 17
  unfamiliar area, 22

Hunting ethic
  passing to next generation,
    232
Hunting experience
  bowhunting, 115–118
  first kill experience,
    141–144
  pressured deer, 20
  Stan Potts, 147
  firearm season
    pressure deer, 21
  hunts, 134–136
  muzzleloader, 12–13
  opening weekend of
    Wisconsin firearms
    season, 9–13
  personal, 1–4
  whitetail hunts, 134–136
Hunting permission
  landowner relations, 23–24
Hunting pressure
  deer movement
    to refuge, 44
  levels
    four, 20
    one, 19
    three, 19–20
    two, 19
  varieties and levels, 18
  whitetail adaptations, 14
  whitetail response, 38
Hunting success, 14
  and hard work, 16
  and scouting, 109
  camouflage
    for still-hunting success,
      161
  from scouting, 53–81

natural cover
   for still-hunting, 161
Hunts
   hunting experience
     experiences, 134–136
Hyngstrom, Scott, 39–41
   deer's evasive tactics, 51

I
Illinois public land legend,
   147–155
Iowa
   change during season, 18
   public hunting area, 26
   whitetail hunting, 17

J
Jacket, 137
Journal
   importance, 24
   shed hunters, 72
   stand site
     best wind for hunting areas,
     100
     entry points, 75
   used in scouting, 72
Judgment errors, 228

K
Kisky, Don, 68
Kisky, Kandi, 68
Knife, 138
Knowledge
   tracking, 128–136

Kroll, James, 34–36, 42, 52
   deer's evasive tactics, 51

L
Ladder stands, 106
Landowners
   hunters permission, 225
   relationships, 208
     hunting permission, 23–24
   suburban, 205
Large drives, 180–188
   organization, 181
Layering clothing, 110
Lead doe, 215
Level Four pressure
   hunter adaptation, 22
Limited-entry hunt, 164
Location shifts, 38–42
Lost hunters
   tales about, 171–172
Low-impact hunting, 210
Lucas, Rob, 202–222
   photo, 207
Lyme disease, 204–205

M
Manufactured portable ground
   blinds, 108
MapCard, 66
Maptech
   website and phone number,
   66
Marchinton, Larry
   telemetry study, 48–50
Marginal shots, 220
Marum, Jordan, 9–10

Marum, Ted, 9–11, 188, 190, 194–195
Mature bucks
and dominance
refuges, 45–46
breeding behaviors, 45–46
natural behavior
learned survival
mechanism, 35
vs. younger animal, 130
Mega-Tarsal Plus, 78
Mental toughness, 148
Metro Bowhunters Resource
Base (MBRB), 219–220
Metro challenge, 199–222
Metro hunts, 164
Midday movement pattern, 35
Migratory deer
in refuge, 43
Mini-drives, 175–180
Minnesota, 199
Minnesota Department of
Natural Resources
(MDNR), 43–45
researchers, 31
Missouri Department of
Conservation, 46
Mock scrape, 78
Moon phase
causing pattern shift, 37
Mossy Oaks pants, 160
Motion cameras
photo, 79
using, 80
Movement. *See* Deer,
movement
Moving
too quickly, 122

Muzzleloader
Dakota
location shift, 40
hunting experience, 12–13

N
Natural cover
for still-hunting success, 161
Natural selection, 45
Nebraska's Desoto National
Wildlife Refuge, 39
Next generation
passing hunting ethic to,
232
Nocturnal movement, 34
Noise, 187
North American Shed Hunters
Club, 68
Nudging deer, 184

O
Observation, 190
Off-season reconnaissance, 60
Off-season scouting, 62–67
Older does
fooling, 215
Optics
essential for still-hunter, 162

P
Paint
face, 166
Pants. *See also* Clothing
Mossy Oaks, 160
Patience, 123

and stand hunters, 89
and still-hunting, 115
Patterns, 134. *See also* Deer,
    patterns
    establishing, 73
    shifting, 34–38
Permanent stands, 106
    safety, 107
Persistence
    tracking, 128–136
Pheasant hunters, 39
Portable ladder steps, 105
Portable stands, 10
Post-season scouting trips
    observations, 60
Potts, Stan
    bowhunting
        personal experiences, 147
    photo, 148
Pressure
    accessing, 24
    assessing
        during hunt, 25
        importance, 26–27
    defining and assessing, 9–27
    evaluating level, 21
Pressure levels
    assessing property, 22
Pressured deer, 18
    doubling back through
        drivers, 172–173
    movement, 86, 90–94
Pressured deer ethic
    adoption, 223–233
Prevailing winds, 150
Printed log
    stand site
        best wind for hunting areas,
            100

Private property, 225
    secure permission, 145
Public areas
    archery-only area, 148
    bowhunting, 145, 147
Public opinion, 217
Pushers
    bowhunting tactics, 165–
        166
    bush, 185

R
Radio collar, 32
    does, 39
Realtree shirt, 160
Reconnaissance. *See also*
    Scouting
    off-season, 60
Recreation, 231
Reeve, Pat, 181–188
Refuge effect, 42–46
Remington 760, 137
Remote camera pictures
    used to obtain information,
        80
Remote cameras
    to discover deer, 76
Remote-sensing cameras, 77
Ridge-running bucks, 192
Root, Brian, 46–48
    deer's evasive tactics, 51
Rope, 138
Rub lines, 64
Rubber boots, 214
Rut
    deer
        movement per day, 48
        midday movement, 36

S

Saddles in ridge
  travel areas, 42
Safety
  drives, 195–197
  still hunters, 136–139
Safety harness, 107
Safety mindset, 196
Sanctuaries
  establishing, 94–99
    definition, 94–95
    management strategy, 95
Scent
  estrous, 78
Scent Eliminator spray, 79
Scent Wick, 78
Scent-Lok clothing, 214
Scent-reducing shower, 78
Scents, 78
Science
  and pressured deer, 29–52
Scouting, 24, 25, 53–81, 145
  before hang stands, 93
  bowhunting tactics, 165
  entry and exit trails reaching
    stand, 154
  for travel routes, 91–92
  importance, 149
  in-season, 58–62
  limited by time, 163
  need for, 56–58
  off-season, 62–67
  post-season, 58–62
  spring, 62–67
  suburban hunting
    opportunities, 210–212
  summer and early fall, 74
  time needed, 81
  to determine stand

type and location, 109
travel routes, 93
using aerial photos, 150
Scrapes
  mock, 78
  photo, 158
  shed antlers, 78
  Ultimate Scrape Dripper, 78
Security covers, 94
Sedentary deer
  in refuge, 43
Sharing woods, 231
Shed
  clue to identifying a buck's
    core area, 70
Shed antler hunting
  springtime activity, 69
Shed antlers, 68
  scrape, 78
Shed hunters, 68
  notes and journal, 72
Shed hunting, 229
  used to obtain information,
    80
Shirt
  chamois, 137
Short-duration hunt, 164
Shower
  scent-reducing, 78
Sign
  ignoring, 10, 13
Simon, Dennis, 43–45
  deer's evasive tactics, 51
Site tenacity, 43
Skill
  tracking, 128–136
Small, Kevin, 98, 99
Special Golden Estrous, 78
Special- or limited-entry hunts

bowhunting, 145
Spiegl, John, 58–60
Spoor
reading, 130
Sport
vs. way of life, 17
Spotting scope, 75
Spray
Scent Eliminator, 79
Spring scouting, 62–67
Spy games, 76
Stalking, 153–154
deer, 120
Stand hunter
gear and safety considerations
for, 104–110
Stand hunting
case for, 86–90
for pressured deer, 88–89
photo, 87
purpose and safety, 88
Stand site
improving, 101
Stand(s). *See also* individual types
approaching technique,
152–153, 212
climbing, 106
hang-on type, 104
important, 151
ladder, 106
permanent, 106
safety, 107
portable, 10
types, 104
Stand-hunting tactics, 83–111
Stand-site preparation, 67
Standards
ethical, 220, 231
violations, 228

Standers, 185–186
approach to hunt, 166
placement, 191, 194
situated, 189
State game departments
urban hunts, 218–219
Stealth
personified, 122–128
Still-hunting, 120, 122–128
and tracking techniques,
113–139
areas
characteristics, 159–160
bowhunting tactics, 159
gear, 136–139
mental requirements, 116
mindset, 114–115
safety, 136–139
viewed as, 118–119
Still-hunts
bowhunting, 157
Stop-and-stare, 83–84
Suburban hunting
opportunities
bowhunting, 145
scouting, 210–212
treestands, 211
Suburban landowners, 205
Suburban whitetails
sophistication, 214
Suburban/metro challenge,
199–222
Suburban/metro hunts, 164
Success. *See also* Hunting
success
and hard work, 16
from scouting, 53–81
Summer deer
observing, 75

Summer reconnaissance
    missions, 152
Survival behavior
    fawn, 44
Swamp drive, 169, 170

T
Tagging, 224
Telemetry collars, 33
Telemetry study, 39
    deer ability to run or hide,
        46–48
    deer hunting with hounds,
        48–50
    on deer living
        in state game refuge, 43
Terrain
    changes, 67
    importance of, 160
Time
    and scouting, 57
Tolerance, 228
Topo maps
    from your PC, 66
    importance of, 65–66
    studying, 165
    use of, 163
    what to look for, 67
Tracking, 127
    and Dick Bernier, 119
    buck *vs.* doe, 130
    bucks, 131
    freshness, 132
    importance, 121
    in water, 132
    skill, knowledge, persistence,
        128–136

Trail's End #307, 78
Travel corridors, 212
    stand hunting, 166
Travel routes, 90–94
    classic
        types, 92
    photo, 97
    whitetails
        for cover, 91
Treatment
    of other hunters, 231
Treestands. *See also* Stand(s)
    approaches
        unique, 100
    effectiveness, 120
    hunting
        example, 119
    options, 106
    suburban hunting, 211
Trophy
    everyman's, 6
Trophy-caliber bucks
    drives, 174
Two-man still-hunt, 178–179

U
Ultimate Scrape Dripper, 78
Unchecked herd growth, 204
Underwear, 137
Unsafe behavior
    correcting, 196
Urban bucks
    photo, 219
Urban hunts
    state game departments,
        218–219

V

Vaznis, Bill, 154–162

Venison
donation program, 209

Veteran bucks
disappearing act, 193

W

Walking
and still-hunting, 115
need for, 56

Walking trails, 214

Water
sources, 67
tracking, 132

Weather patterns, 150
causing pattern shift, 37

Whitetail adaptations
to hunting pressure, 14

Whitetail deer. *See* Deer

Whitetail habitat
looking for, 61

Whitetail hunters

fellowship, 2

Whitetail hunting
sport *vs.* way of life, 17

Whitetail hunts
experiences, 134–136

Whittington, Gordon, 52

Wildlife Research Center, Inc.,
80

Wind
direction, 124, 150
and hunting, 92, 152
hunter's scent, 165
prevailing, 150
stand site
best wind for hunting areas,
100

Wisconsin
whitetail hunting, 3, 9 13,
17

Woods
sharing, 231

Woods, Grant, 38

Woody Max, 137

Wool clothing, 137